The
POLYNESIAN TATTOO
Handbook

TattooTribes.com

2011

TABLE OF CONTENTS

Mate atu he tetekura, ara mai he tetekura

''When a fern frond dies, another will take its place''
"Life continues in our children"

FOREWORD

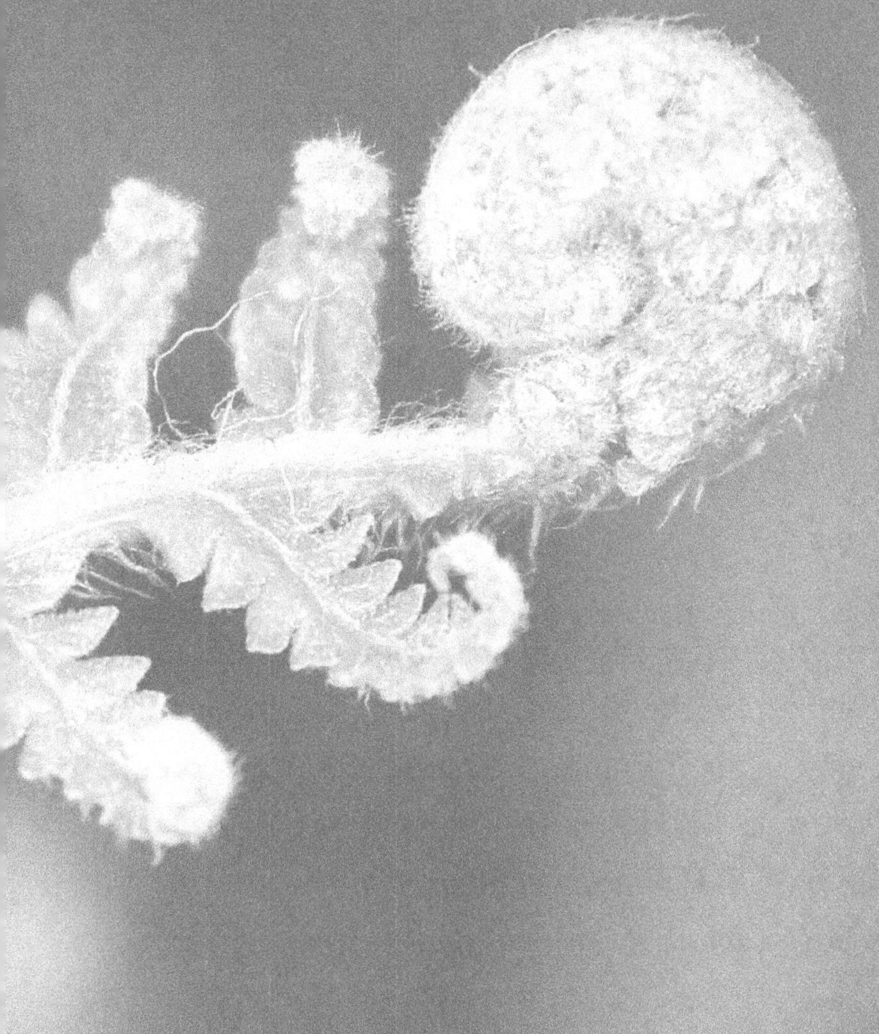

"Mate atu he tetekura, ara mai he tetekura"
—**When a fern frond dies, another will take its place**:
Life continues in our children.

Polynesia is a subregion of Oceania, comprising of a large grouping of over 1,000 islands scattered over the central and southern Pacific Ocean, within a triangle that has New Zealand, Hawaii and Easter Island as its corners. The people who inhabit the islands of Polynesia are termed Polynesians and they share many similar traits including language, culture and beliefs.

Polynesian languages may actually vary slightly from each other, or even a great deal, depending on the distance between the groups of islands and the frequency of their contacts. There are some words which are basically the same throughout all Polynesian languages, reflecting the deepest core of all Polynesian cultures.
Two emblematic ones are *moana* (ocean) and *mana* (spiritual force, energy).
It's interesting to note how similar these two words are and this should not be a surprise once we understand the relation between Polynesian cultures and the ocean.
The ocean guarantees life.

It's also the place of birth and rest.

It means abundance, prosperity and protection, being as vital to man as the air we breathe.

Polynesian tattoos reflect this in a strong way.

Be it in traditional style with more stylized and geometrical patterns only or in modern style (more figurative, like the style presented in this book), sea creatures play a great part in such tattoos. Sharks, mantas, bonitos, sea urchins ... each of them acquires a meaning related to its inner nature and embodies that meaning passing it on to the bearer of the tattoo.

Polynesian tattoos thus become a way to tell stories about their owners (to the extent of becoming a figurative identity card in the case of Maori face tattooing), or a way to give them strength, protection or powers from the bond created with other creatures.

Another important element to be considered is represented by the *aumakua*. An *aumakua* is an entity having supernatural powers (usually a deified ancestor or a spirit), which appears to men usually in the form of an animal, to give them advice, omens and sometimes punishments.

In the case of deified ancestors, families will maintain in time a special relation to their specific animals, which can often be sharks, turtles, rays or other sea creatures.

The attitude towards *aumakua* varies greatly from island to island: some regard tattooing their own *aumakua* as a good omen and a guarantee of protection, whilst others consider them *tapu* (sacred, but also forbidden) and therefore avoid having them tattooed on their bodies.

The role of the *aumakua* is not so different from the totemic animals of Native Americans.

They bring messages and guide and protect us. We must learn their lesson and respect them in order to preserve the bond with them and be protected.

Respect for Nature and her creatures plays an important role in Polynesian cultures and so do balance and union to everything around us.

All this must be taken into consideration when preparing a Polynesian inspired design.

For a *strictly* traditional design a native *tafuga* (tattoo master) should be addressed since the old way of tattooing gets handed from master to disciple and involves far more knowledge than what could be incorporated into a book.

The style of tattooing varies from island to island depending on how much the different traditions have evolved from the original common designs derived supposedly from a former Pacific archeological culture known as Lapita.

▼ ▼ ▼ ▼ ▼ ▼ ▼ ▼ ▼ ▼ ▼ ▼ ▼ ▼ ▼

Traditional styles closer to the origins consist mainly of straight lines and rely heavily on the repetition of a few basic patterns, whose meaning is often forgotten, or at least very controversial.

Nice examples of these geometrical styles are found in Samoan and Hawaiian tattoo traditions, or in tattoos from Palau, Fiji, Tonga, just to name a few.

Maori and Marquesan tattoos instead are rich in rounded elements and share a more figurative style. In the case of the Marquesas Islands we have basically two styles, with the one from Hiva Oa being the most figurative one and also the most used at present.

Tattooing has always been considered a sacred process, a ritual to show the world one's courage, lineage and deeds, as well as a means of communication to the gods.

Tattoo masters were very important people since they knew the meaning of symbols and motifs and how to relate them to create a meaningful work of art personal to each man or woman. They passed their knowledge "vertically", which means from father to son, from master to disciple, without spreading it widely, due to its sacred nature.

Unfortunately this and the prohibitions following to European colonization caused a serious loss of this knowledge.

We still have record of many motifs and elements, but very few of them can be associated to a specific meaning beyond doubt.

In a few cases we can get some help from other mediums like *Kapa* cloth painting: designs used for tattooing have often been used on other mediums too and we have records about them, we know their names (very similar to their corresponding tattoo versions), their symbology and sometimes their meaning, but we can't unfortunately assume they are always the same.

On this account this book does not focus on a specific style.

It does collect symbols, motifs and elements from different Oceanic cultures and styles, selecting the ones that are most widely known and used; since the same symbols can have different meanings in different cultures, we will list here the main ones along with notes reporting the most frequently associated symbology.

A particular focus is given to their placement on the body, the relation between different symbols and how to choose them to create a meaningful design going beyond bare aesthetics to tell a story, with real life examples and case studies explained in detail.

We must now open a brief parenthesis about writings and letters incorporated into Polynesian designs.

Since Polynesian cultures did not have written alphabets, traditional Polynesian tattoos did not include writings.

How can we deal with them?

How can they become part of a Polynesian styled design seamlessly, without looking out of place?

The solution we adopted is called *maorigrams*.
The appendix of the book deals with them, with step by step instructions explaining how they can be created.

Ko main kai atu ko maru kai mai ka ngohengohe

"Give as much as you take and everything will be fine"
"Don't be selfish, live a balanced life"

"Ko main kai atu ko maru kai mai ka ngohengohe"
—***Give as much as you take and everything will be fine***:
Don't be selfish, live a balanced life.

Placement on the body plays an important role in Polynesian tattooing. There are several elements that inherit a specific meaning based on their placement and even the relation between elements and their relative positioning has an influence on the meaning of a tattoo.

Humans are children of Rangi (Heaven) and Papa (Earth), which were once united. Man's quest is to find that union again and the body can ideally be seen as a link between Rangi and Papa, where the upper part is related to the spiritual world and to Rangi whilst the lower part is related to the material world and to Papa, similarly to most cultures worldwide. The placements of some elements on the body, such as genealogy tracks on the back of the arms, suggest that the back may be related to the past and the front to the future.
Gender-wise, left is usually associated to female and right to male.
A tattoo should then reflect balance and union, containing elements relating to both Rangi and Papa; the position of tattoos on the body often followed a balancing rule too: a tattoo on the left leg could be matched by another one on the right arm and so on.

Let's see the body in detail:

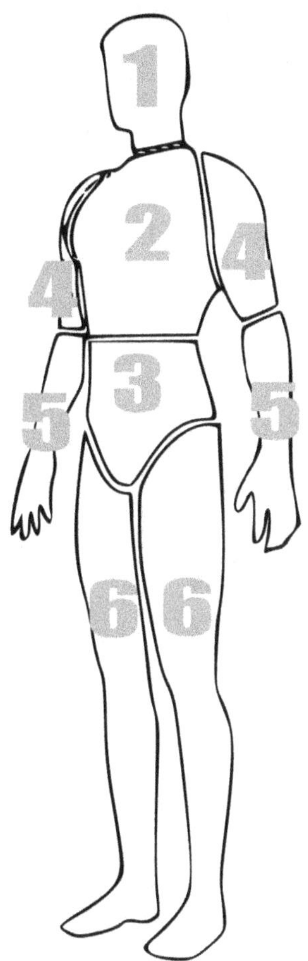

1. Head

It's our contact to Rangi and as such it is related to **spirituality**, **knowledge**, **wisdom** and **intuition**.

Maori people gave great importance to head and face and their facial tattoo, called *Tā Moko*, represented an identity card, reporting information about a man, his status and deeds, his ancestors and their deeds too. That's the reason why copying a facial tattoo is considered greatly offensive: it's like stealing someone's identity, claiming that his very own history belongs to someone else.

2. Higher trunk

Above the navel onto the chest.
Related to **generosity**, **sincerity**, **honour**, **joy** and **reconciliation**. It is placed between Rangi and Papa and in order to have harmony between them, balance must exist in this area.

3. Lower trunk

From thighs to navel.
This part of the body relates to **life's energy**, **courage**, **sexuality and procreation**, **independence**.
Thighs in particular relate to **strength** and **marriage**.
The belly is where *mana* originates and the navel represents **independence** due to the symbolical meaning associated to the cut of the umbilical cord.
One note should be added about this: independence has a positive

value in Polynesian society as in almost any other, but individualism has not. All people depending on the sea for living know the importance of sociality. Polynesian people built all their culture around this. Family becomes thus a larger group, where also neighbours and friends play an important role. A famous word to define this widened family comes from Hawaii: it's *'Ohana* which indicates the familiar group of people including relatives, akins, friends and all the important ones who cooperate in growing the children, feeding and teaching them.

4. Upper arms and shoulders

Shoulders and upper arms above the elbow are associated to **strength** and **bravery** and they relate to warriors, chiefs.
The Maori word *kikopuku* used to designate this part is the union of the words *kiko* (flesh, body) and *puku* (swollen). *Puku* as a prefix or suffix is also used as an intensifier of the word it qualifies, enforcing the idea of strong arms.

5. Lower arms and hands

From below the elbow; the same word is used to refer both to arm and hand.
This part of the body relates to **creativity**, **creation**, **making things**.

6. Legs and feet

The same word is used to refer both to leg and foot.

Legs and feet represent **moving forward**, **transformation** and **progress**. They are also related to **separation** and **choice**.

The feet, being our contact with Papa, Mother Nature, are also related to **concreteness** and **material matters**.

Joints

Joints often represent **union, contact**.

If we look at the body as a reflection of society, we can understand why joints, being the points where different bones meet, represent different degrees of relation between individuals: the farer from the head (the chief of the family) the greater the distance in kinship, or the lower the status.

Ankles and wrists represent a **tie** and bracelets placed there (the checkered pattern in primis) often symbolize **committment**.

Knees are often related to chiefs (to kneel before them).

Side note:

traditional positioning should not keep you from placing your tattoos on any part of the body you may feel appropriate for you: we believe a design should be meaningful to his owner before than to anyone else.

O le malie ma le tu'u malie

"Every shark must be paid for"
"There's no free beer"

3 SYMBOLS AND MEANINGS

"O le malie ma le tu'u malie"
—Every shark must be paid for*:*
There's no free beer.

This chapter provides a brief list of the most common symbols and motifs used in tattooing, collected throughout the whole span of Oceania, along with the meanings usually associated to them.

There are many more symbols and motifs than the ones reported here but either their meaning is not known or we can't be reasonably sure about it. Since Oceania has tens of main islands and hundreds of smaller ones, it is almost impossible to associate a univocal meaning to every element. For the same reason it's almost impossible to "read" an existing design because it is strongly related to the decisions and choices of the tattoo artist who designed it, even if the general meaning can still be deduced by the main elements incorporated in it. Great part of the known symbols comes from Marquesan traditions since the most complete record we have of Polynesian tattooing was published in 1928 by Karl von den Steinen based on the notes taken during his expedition to the Marquesas back in 1897-98.

Human figures

Enata

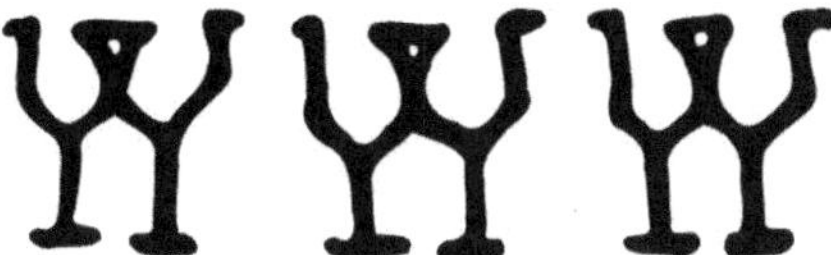

Human figures, or *enata* in Marquesan language, represent men, women and sometimes gods. They can be placed in a tattoo to represent people and their relations: friends, relatives, dear people. Placed upside down they can be used to represent defeated enemies. Here are some examples of *enata* motifs, showing how the symbol evolved from its pictorial representation to the commonly used stylized version:

First simplification:

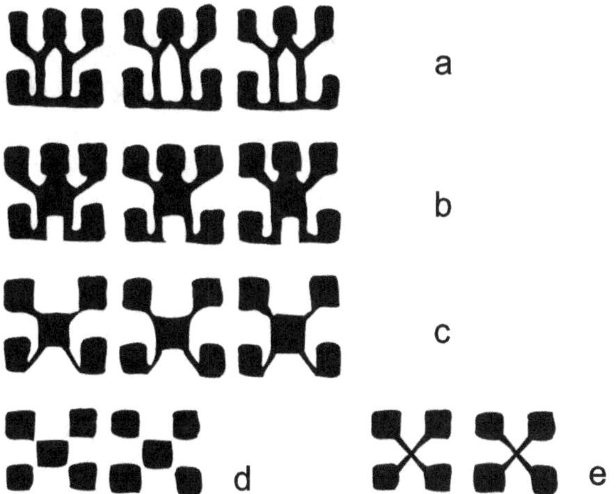

Second simplification:

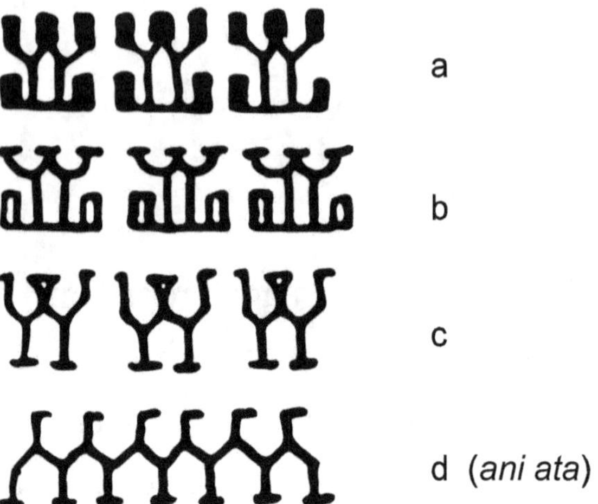

a

b

c

d (*ani ata*)

Overstylized *enata* joined together in a row of people holding hands form the motif called *ani ata*, which translates to "cloudy sky":
Rangi (Heaven) and Papa (Earth) once laid closely embracing each other and their children lived between them in darkness until deified men forced them apart by pushing Rangi up to let the light in. This concept of a row related to the sky is present throughout all Polynesian languages and a row of *enata* in a semicircle is commonly used to represent the sky as well as the ancestors guarding upon their descendants:

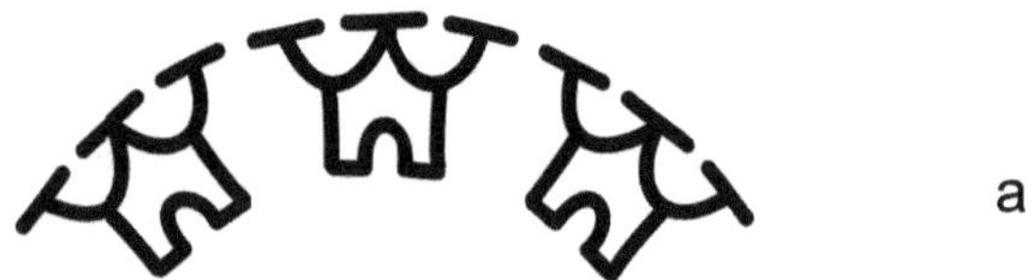

a

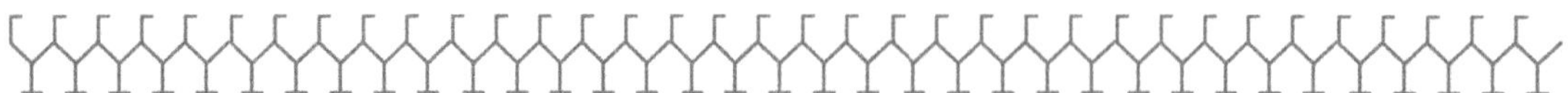

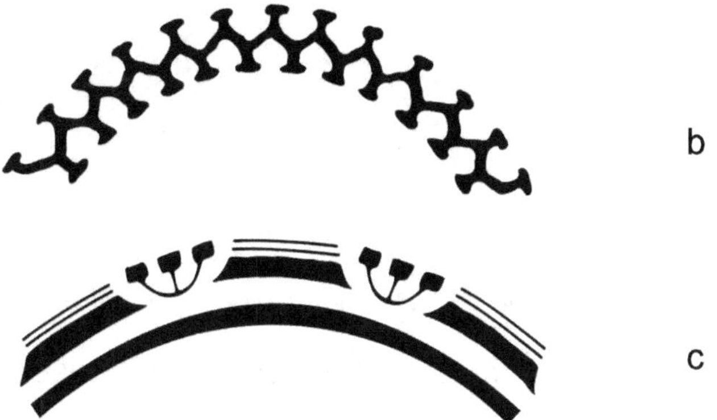

b

c

A human figure coupled with a facing one is traditionally used to represent marriage:

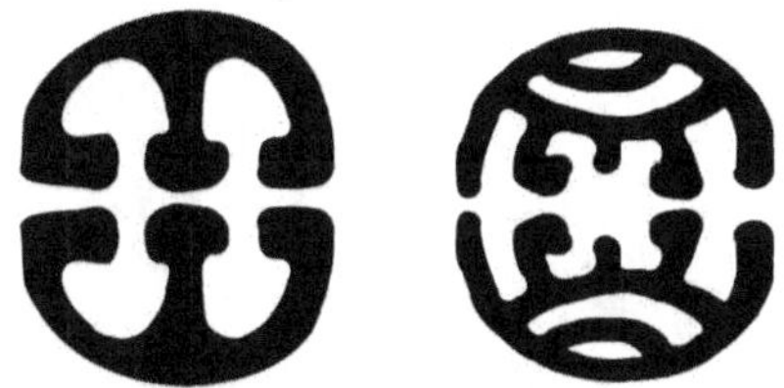

Man and woman are sometimes differentiated, especially when representing a couple:

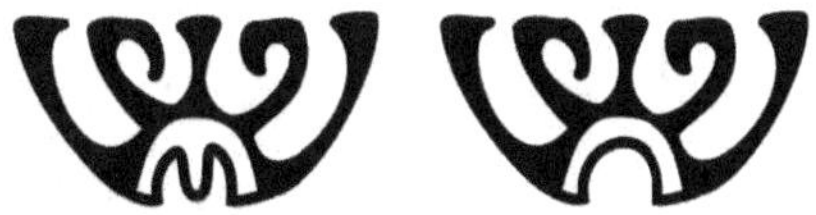

Other versions of human figures are often used to represent a warrior, especially when holding a spear above the head (see also the next entry, warrior):

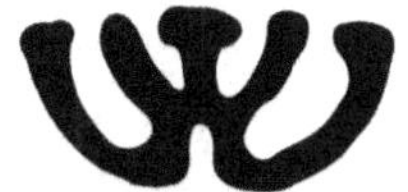

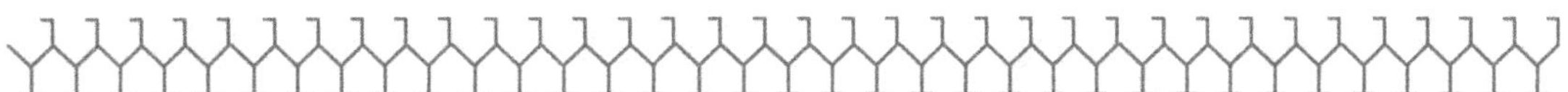

Warrior

Kena

Kena is a Marquesan mythological hero and the same name is given to the symbol representing him, which is often used to represent a warrior:

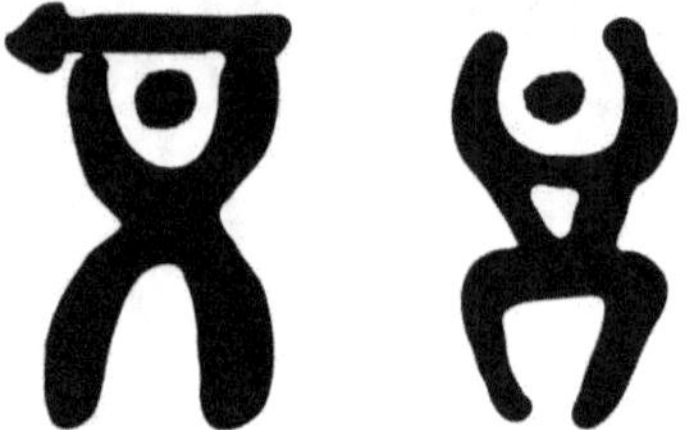

From *kena* originate the next simplified motifs, overstylized in version b where just torso, head and arms are shown:

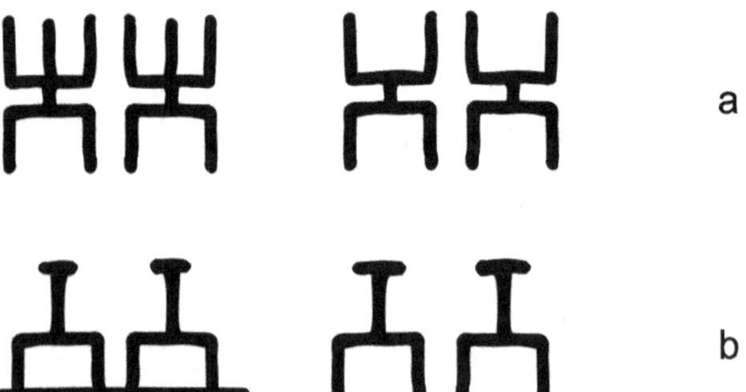

a

b

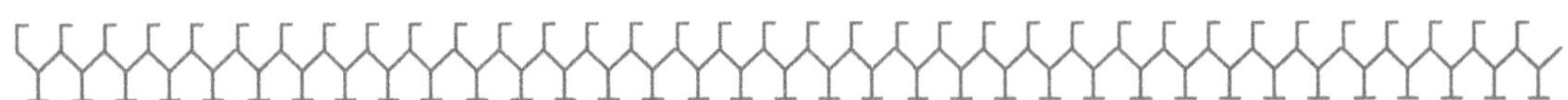

Spear heads

Another classic symbol used to represent a warrior is the spear:

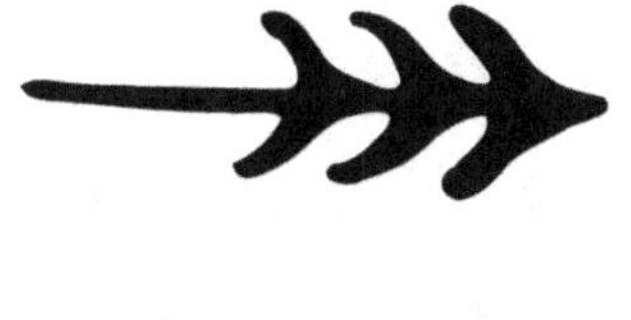

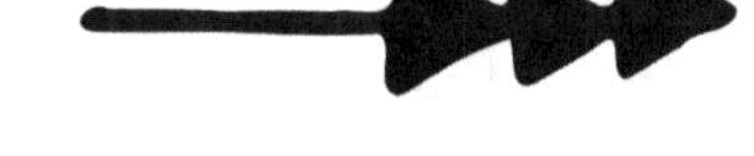

which is often stylized as a row of spearheads, a few variants of which are listed below:

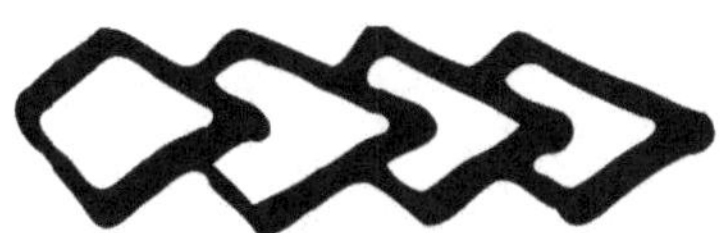

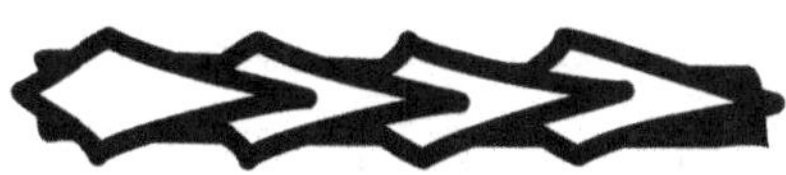

Spear heads are symbolic for sharp items too and can be used to represent the sting of some rays and male animals.

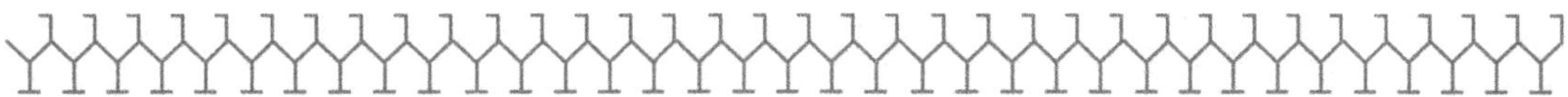

Adze

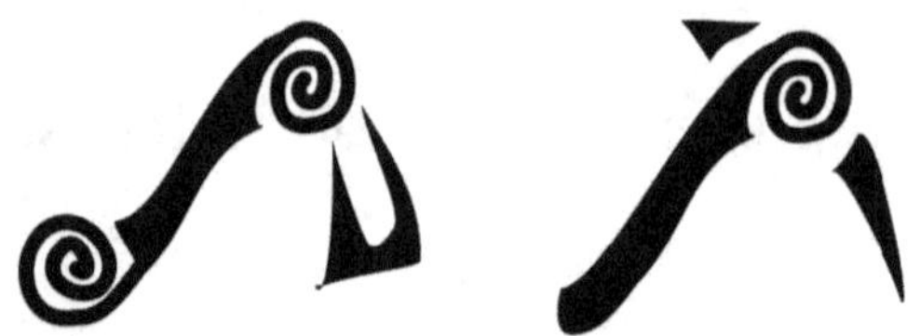

Stone adzes served on many purposes and war was just one of them. They were used to carve canoes, as a baton held by orators and to build the marae, the long houses used as the meeting place of the community.

They symbolize **craftmanship**, **operosity**, **authority** and **force** (both physical and moral), **overcoming obstacles**.

Centipede

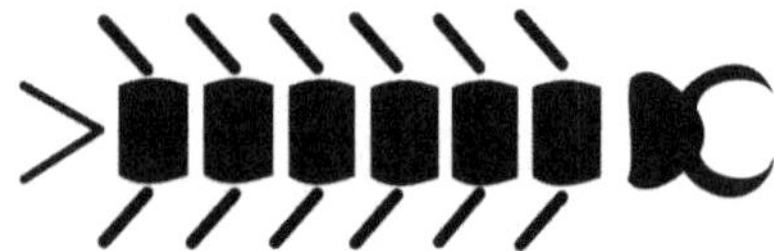

Even if the centipede has no poisonous sting, its symbolism recalls closely the scorpion's one. Its aggressive nature and attitude caused it to symbolize the **fighting spirit**, **warriors**.

Related meanings are **determination**, **rebellion**. The following two images are, respectively, a stylization of the centipede and a traditional motif representing it.

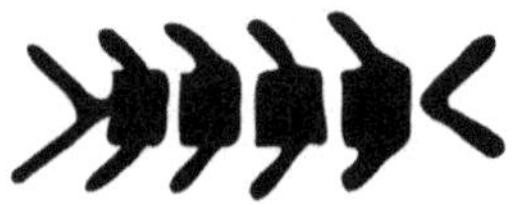

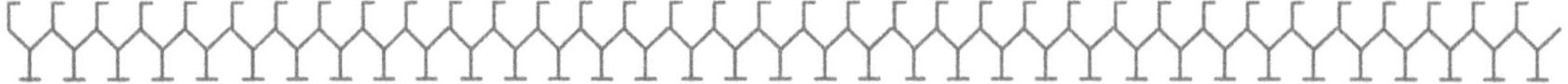

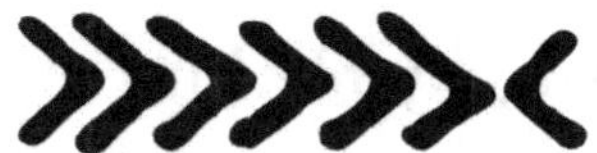

Mere

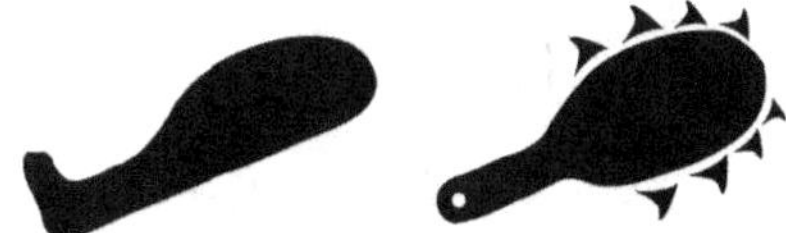

Mere are flat short clubs used in war mainly by chiefs. They were handed through the generations and sometimes exchanged on solemn occasions. On this account they represent the **chief**, **honor**, **respect**, **nobility**, **greatness** and all those traits that a respected chief should have.

Lizard

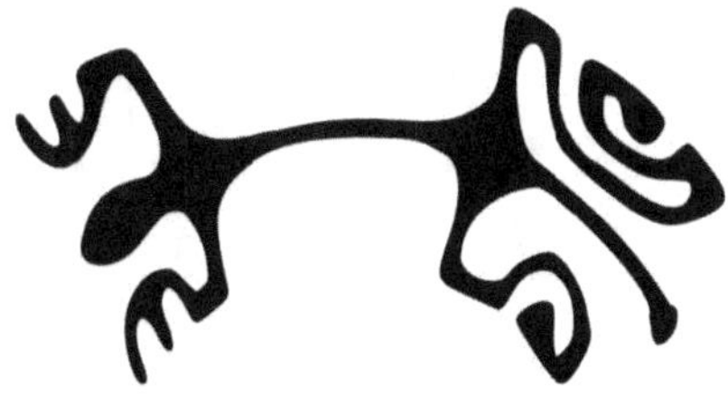

Lizards and geckos are called *mo'o* or *moko* and they play an important role in Polynesian myths.

Gods (*atua*) and minor spirits often appeared to men under the

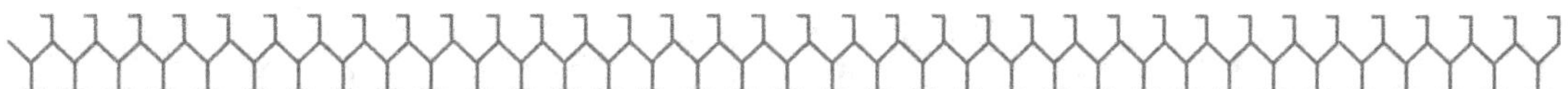

form of lizards and this may explain why the stylized element used to represent the lizard is very similar to the stylized symbol used for man.

Lizards are powerful creatures who can bring **good luck**, **communicate to the gods** and **access the invisible world** as well as bring death and bad omens to unrespectful people.

In Australian Aboriginal culture lizards represent **regeneration**, **transformation** and **survival through hardships**.

In Maori culture they are often regarded as **guardians** and a lizard was often buried next to the newly built houses, or carved on their walls, to **keep every disease and evil spirit away** from them.

The following series of motifs shows how, by simplifying the lizard, we reach a design that recalls the stylized *enata* very closely; lizards are considered to be the ancestors of men and this may be another reason for this similarity.

Stylization steps:

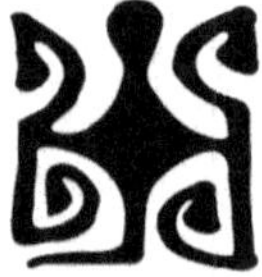

a

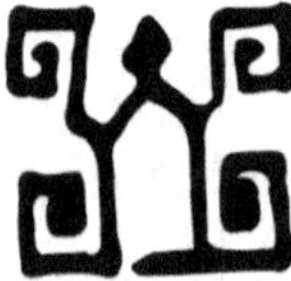

b

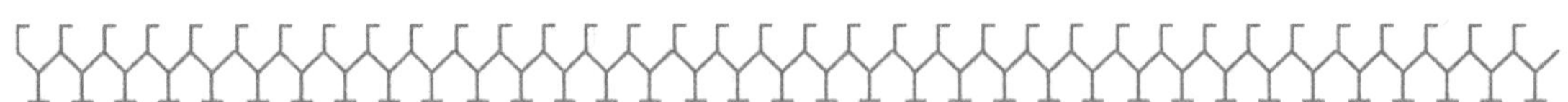

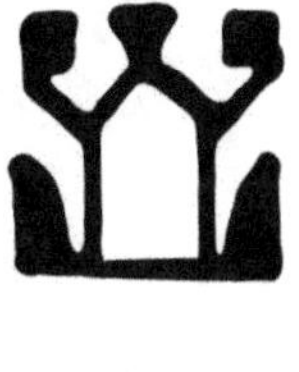

c

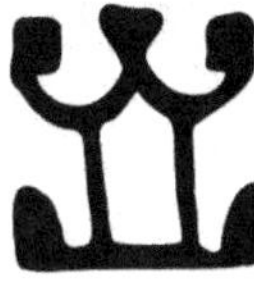

d

Moko is also the name of Maori facial tattooing, which is considered sacred too and whose name may derive by early designs, which featured lizards as signs of divine descent and thus were adopted by chiefs. Lizard motifs on the face are common to early Hawaiian tattoos too and it's easy to think that navigators knew them when they first left from the home land of Hawaiki to discover the new land of Aotearoa where they later settled. In Maori myths *Tā Moko* is told to have a divine origin and it should not be misused by non-Maori (*pakeha*), who can instead use *kirituhi* designs (literally drawn skin). *Tā Moko* elements are important as much as their positioning, conveying information on the bearer, on his rank and on the rank of his ancestors. *Kirituhi* is just a decorative style that recalls *Tā Moko* and can be applied anywhere and by anyone.

Turtle

The turtle, or *honu*, is another important creature throughout all Polynesian cultures and has been associated to several meanings.

Mostly, sea turtles symbolize **health**, **fertility**, **long life**, **foundation**, **peace**, **rest**, the **navigator**.

The word *hono* designating the turtle in Marquesan language has also other meanings, among which we'll report "to join, to stitch together", which may explain why the turtle also represents **union**, **family** (another explanation may be the fact that sea turtles cross the whole Ocean to reach the shore where they were born and where they'll give birth to their own babies).

The Ocean is the source of life for islanders; the Polynesian sea is rich in all kinds of fish and represents wealth, but it is often the place of rest too. Land and sea are the two halves of the world and the turtle can live in and on both and move from one to the other. On this account the turtle is believed to move between the world of the living and the world beyond and to join and shepherd the departed along their last voyage, taking them safe to their place of rest.

Contrary to what is sometimes believed, turtles drawn upwards

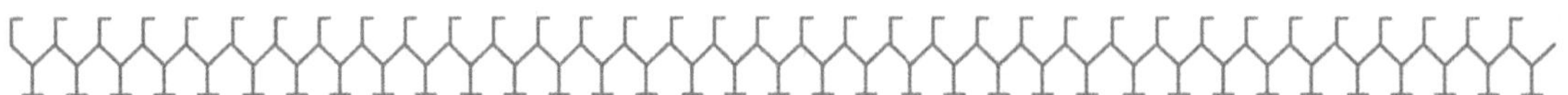

do not imply that they are taking the soul of a dead person to the other world: in Polynesian myths Rangi is where deities and some spirits reside and where the souls of men and women are created before their birth, but not where they usually go after death. That's a western concept that does not reflect pre-contact beliefs.

To represent a dead person safely taken by a turtle to their place of rest, a human figure may be placed on the shell or close to it instead.

Two *enata*-like symbols, like the ones in the next figure, are a traditional way for representing a turtle (notice how they look like the first turtle image from the previous page):

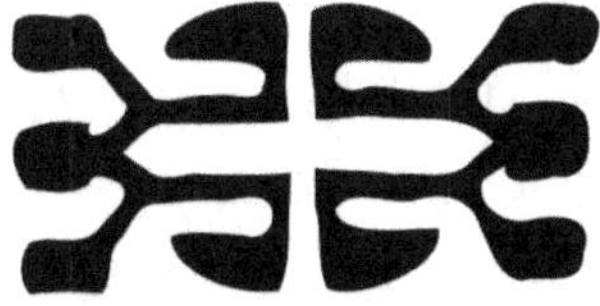

Other patterns are derived by the inlay of the shell, being stylized as in the following samples:

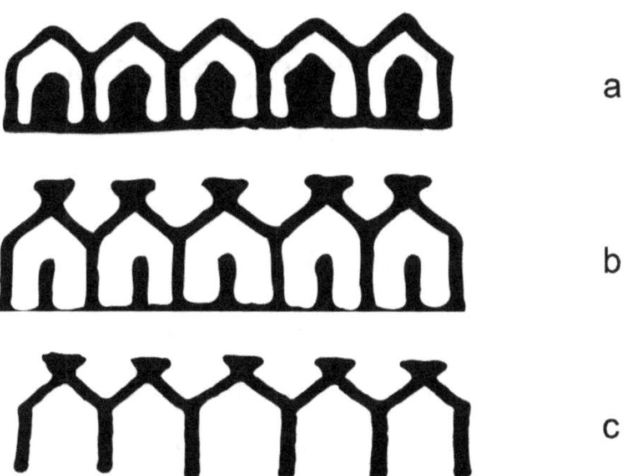

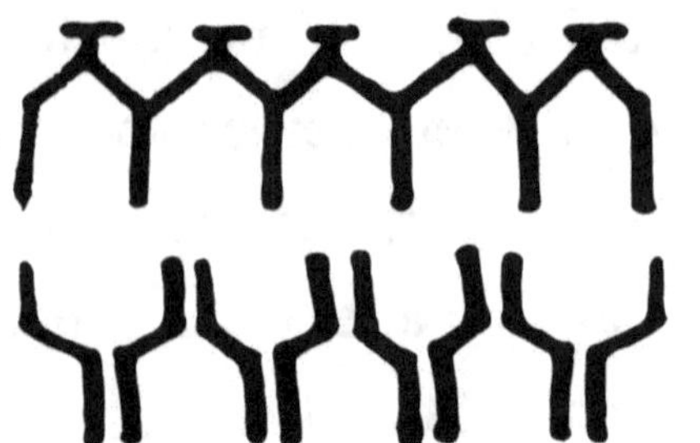

d

e

Fish

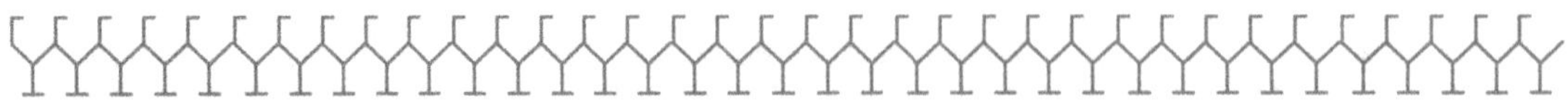

Fish are the main source of food to Polynesian people. They symbolize **wealth**, **plenty**, **prosperity**, **life**.
Specific fish are often identified by stylized motifs representing a specific trait they have, such as teeth for the shark, which appear in most designs and on any part of the body.

A row of shark teeth applied around the ankle has its origin from an Hawaiian legend: once a woman was bitten by a shark on the ankle while swimming. The shark was her aumakua, but he bit her because he didn't recognize her at first. When the woman screamed his name out the shark let her go and apologized for the mistake. He promised he would not repeat the mistake again because the sign of his teeth around her ankle would clearly identify her from that day on.

On this account, a row of shark teeth around the ankle is tattooed for **protection in the water**.

Fish, as symbols of plenty, were also offered to the gods to call their **blessing** on a new house or canoe and fishermen often offered their first fish to the sea god Tangaroa.

Here are some stylizations of fishes:

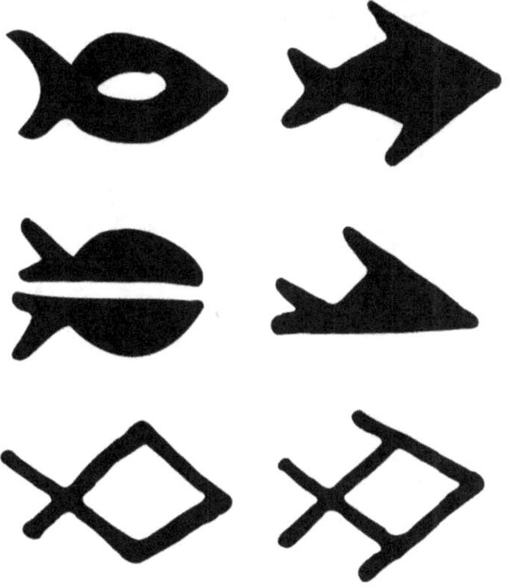

Another pattern coming from Hawaii is made of fish scales, representing **protection**:

fish scales variants

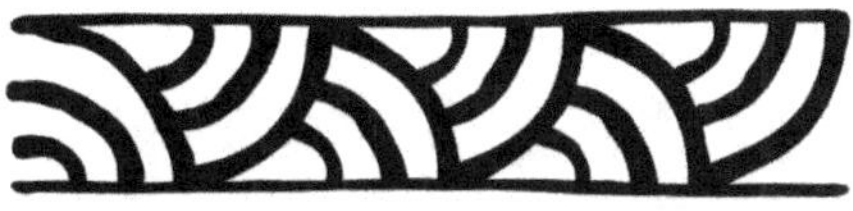

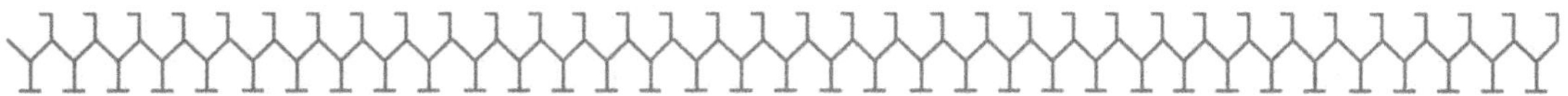

Shark

Shark teeth, or *niho mano*, deserve a space of their own: sharks are one of the favourite forms that *aumakua* choose to appear to man. They represent **protection**, **guidance** and **strength**, **fierceness**, the **warrior**, but they are also symbols of **adaptability** in many cultures. A few samples will show the stylization of shark teeth, both single and doubled:

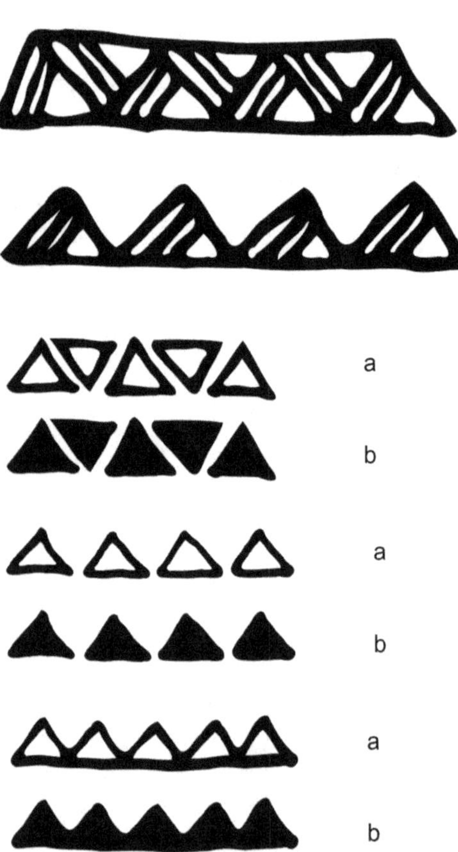

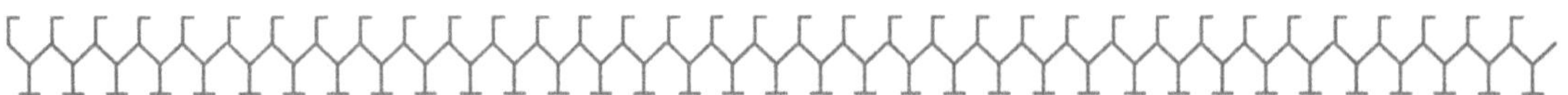

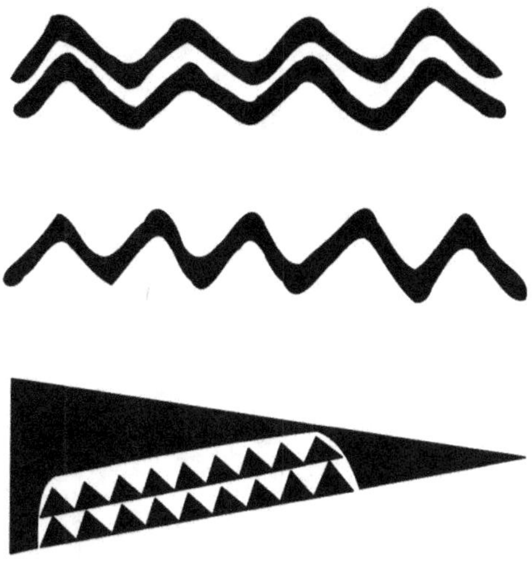

Hammerhead shark

Hammerhead sharks represent **tenacity**, **strength** and **determination** and they are also a symbol of **sociality** since they always move in groups of many individuals.

Here are a few examples of Maori patterns showing the hammerhead shark motif (*mango pare*), from complex patterns to more simple ones:

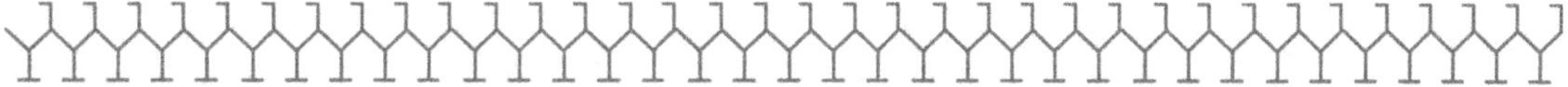

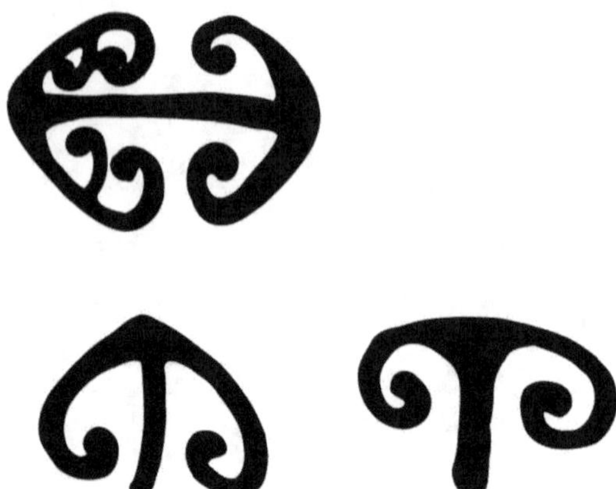

Bonito

A pattern which looks like shark teeth is actually called "bonito tail" or *hiku-atu*. It represents the bonito (a tuna) and it symbolizes **energy**, **agility**, **skill** and **plenty**:

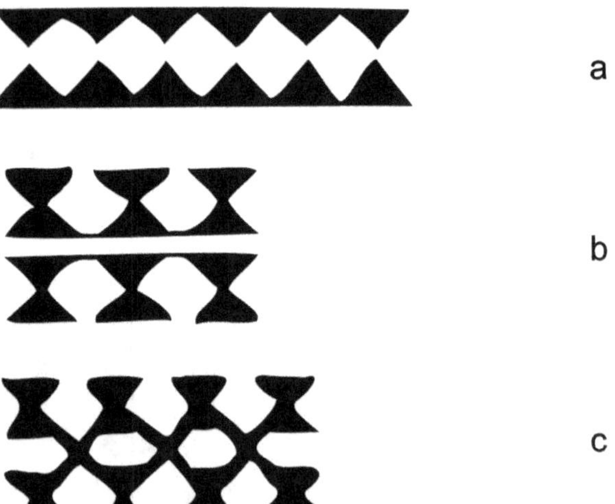

a

b

c

Moray eel

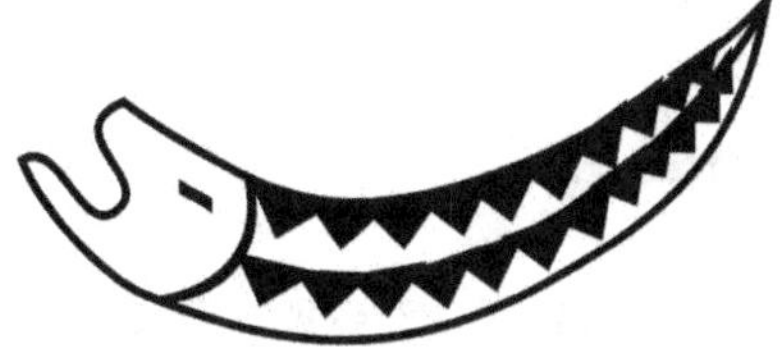

Eels often appear in Polynesian myths as evil spirits. They can live in the sea as well as in fresh waters and many stories are told of eels that tricked and devoured men. They simbolyze **evil spirits**, **adversities, illness**.

Here are two stylizations:

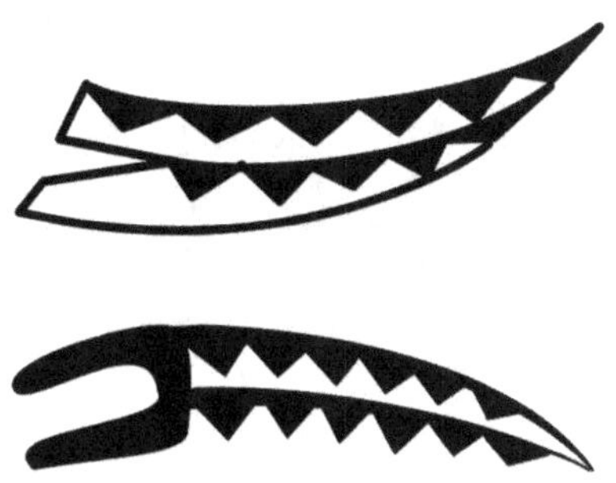

Whale

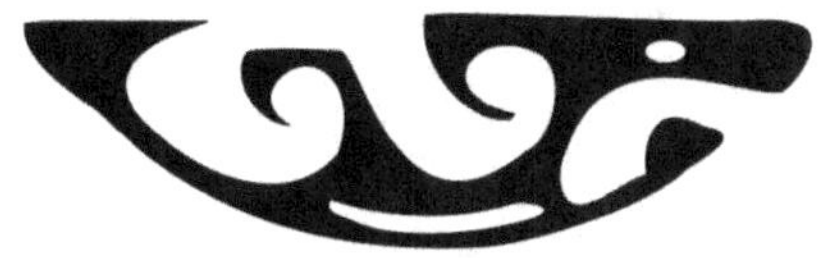

Marquesan
traditional motif

Whales represent **abundance** and, especially when joined by their cubs, **family**, **nurturing**, **care**.

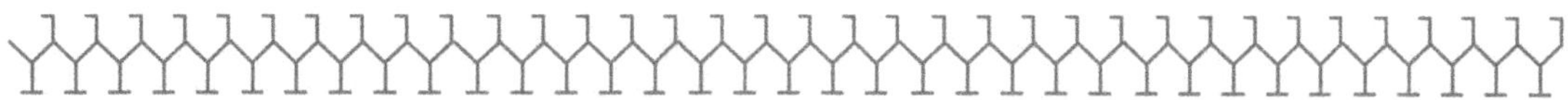

Other sea creatures with a specific meaning:

<u>Dolphins</u> symbolize **playfulness**, **joy**, **friendship**.

<u>Barracudas</u> represent **fierceness**, **determination**, the **warrior**.

<u>Marlins</u> are symbolic of **speed** and **sharp mind**, **heading straight for their goals**.

<u>Mantas</u> and <u>Rays</u> symbolize **elegance**, **freedom**, **wisdom** and **protection**.

<u>Sea urchins</u> have a **stingy and rugged outside, but a soft and delicious inside**. They are also used to symbolize **light in darkness**.

<u>Orcas</u> represent **family protection**, **strength**, **swiftness** and **deadliness**.

<u>Birds</u>

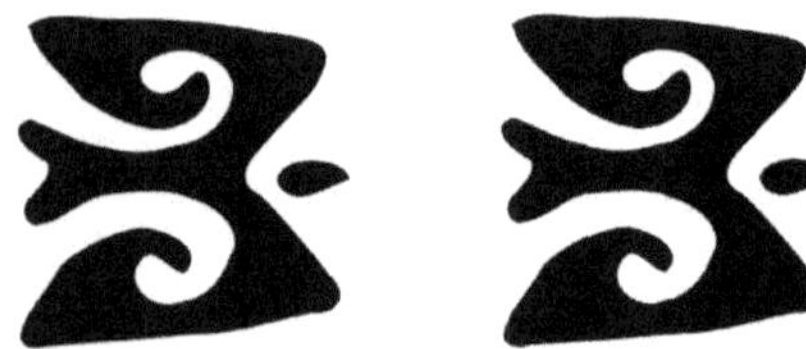

Birds inherit their meanings from their habits and behaviours and appear in many Polynesian proverbs and sayings.

In general they represent **freedom**, the ability to **rise above** earthly

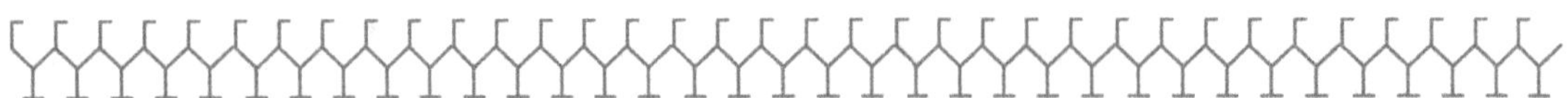

matters to watch the world from a **higher perspective** and they were often considered **messengers** of the *atua*, the gods.

seagull

<u>Frigates</u> are long distance travellers and they symbolize **voyage**, **discovery**.

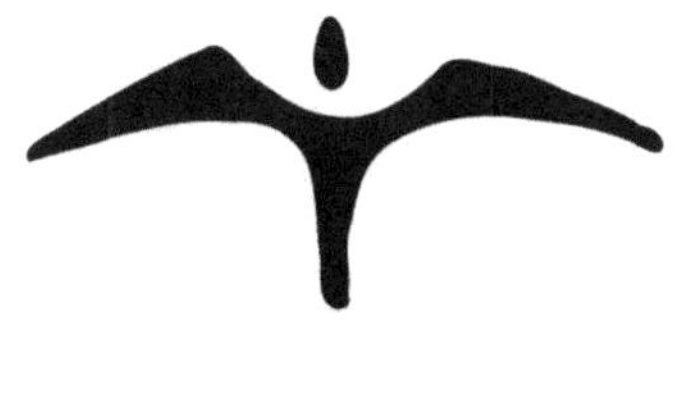

frigates

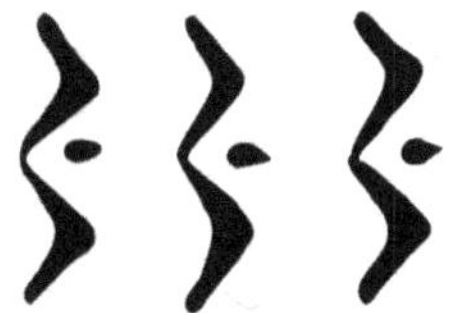

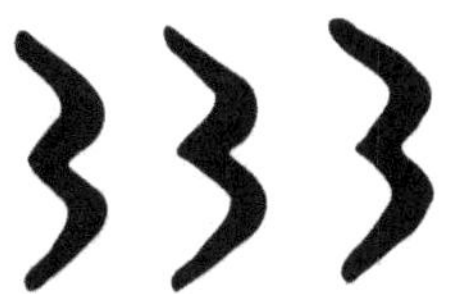

<u>Pigeons</u> were common in the life of Polynesian people and were hunted to integrate the fruits of the land and of the sea. Their habits were studied and earned them their symbolism: pigeons mated for life and when one of them was hurt the mate was reported to fly down to cover her with his wings in order to protect her, even if this may mean to be caught in turn.

On this account the design of two pigeons chasing each other symbolizes **mates, helping each other in times of need**.

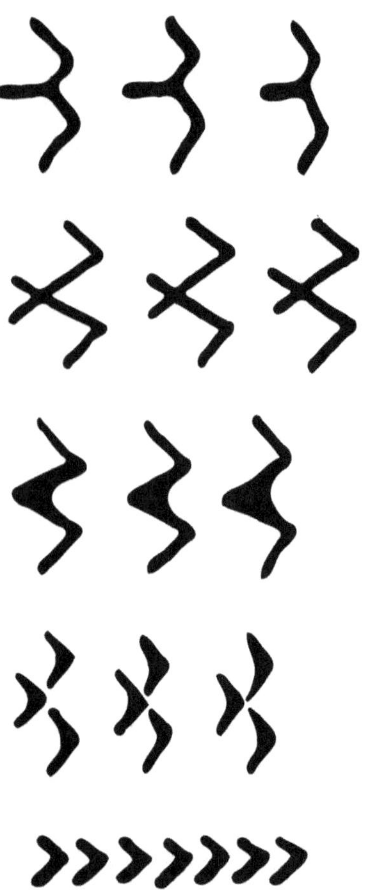

pigeon

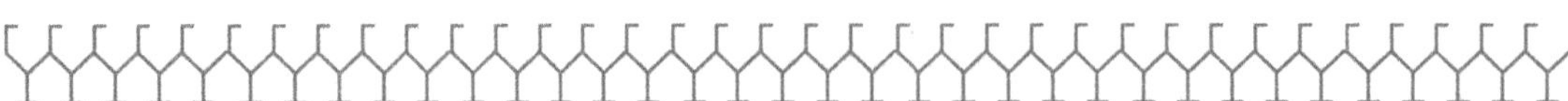

A different bird among a flock of similar ones is used to represent **pride**, **singularity**:

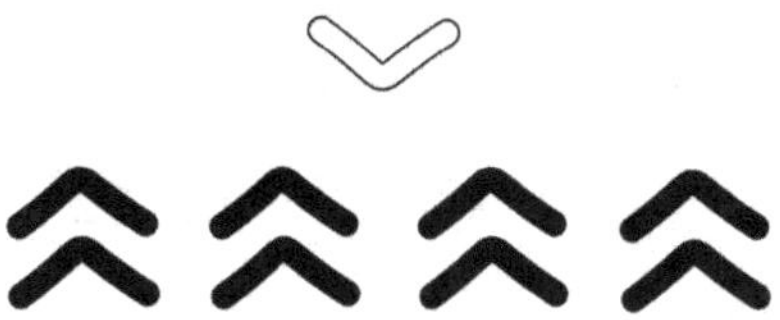

Flying foxes are the biggest bats in the world and they are native of Australia. They are highly social animals living in big communities comprising sometimes thousands of individuals. They feed on fruit and never leave their community even after reaching maturity. They symbolize **community**, **maternal instinct**, but also **operosity** and **hyperactivity**.

The following sample is mutuated from the Samoan traditional tattoo motif called *pe'a*.

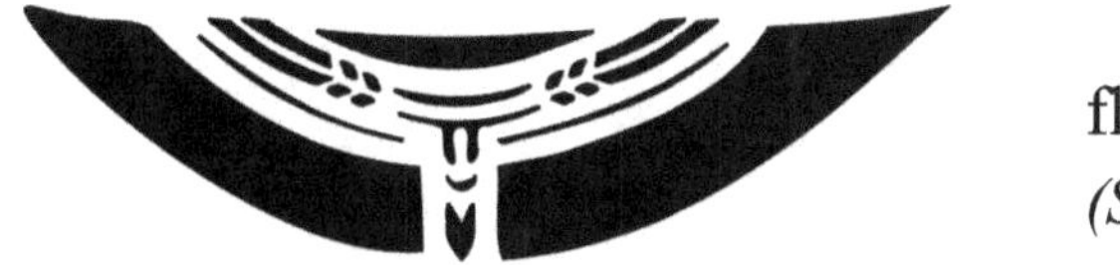

flying fox
(*Samoan trad.*)

In Polynesian designs **fire** is often represented by birds.

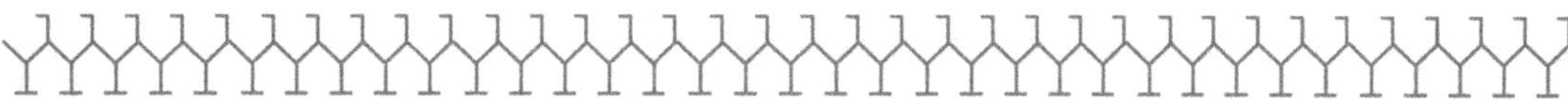

Fishing & hunting

Fishing and hunting were the two main activities in Polynesian life when at peace. Many are the meanings related to these aspects of everyday's life and a **skillful** hunter or fisherman was respected and honored.

Fish hook

The Pacific Ocean has such plenty of fish that just owning fish hooks meant to be wealthy. Fish hooks, or *matau*, are in fact common symbols for **plenty, prosperity, abundance, luck**. When a concept gets caught and held, much like a fish, fish hooks are used to symbolize **knowledge, intelligence** and they can also represent a **promise**.

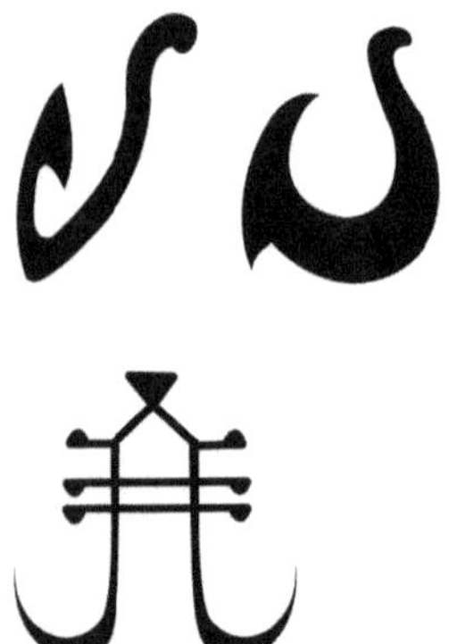

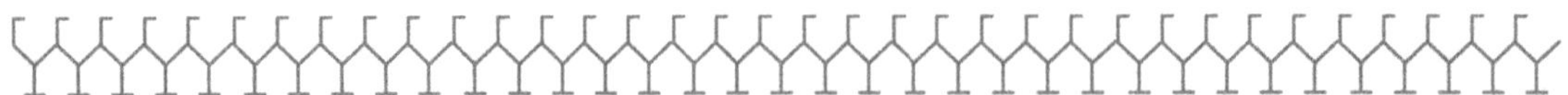

Birds net

When hunting birds, Polynesian people often used special nets they cast or hid between trees where the birds were then forced to fly escaping from the hunters. Nets represent **plenty, solidarity, skill**. Since they are made of several cords woven together to achieve the final result, they symbolize **teamwork, union**. They also represent **generosity** because it was so important in the life of Polynesian people to show generosity towards the less fortunate fishers and hunters: it helps to make the community stronger and makes sure that everyone always has enough to live on; you never know when it will be your turn to have bad luck and you too may need some help, sooner or later.

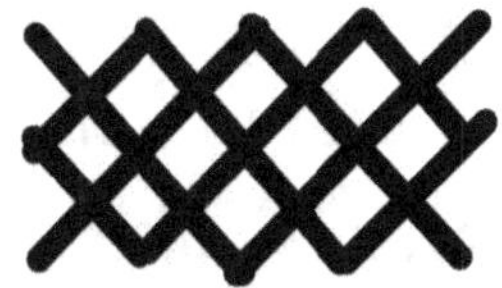

Stylizations:

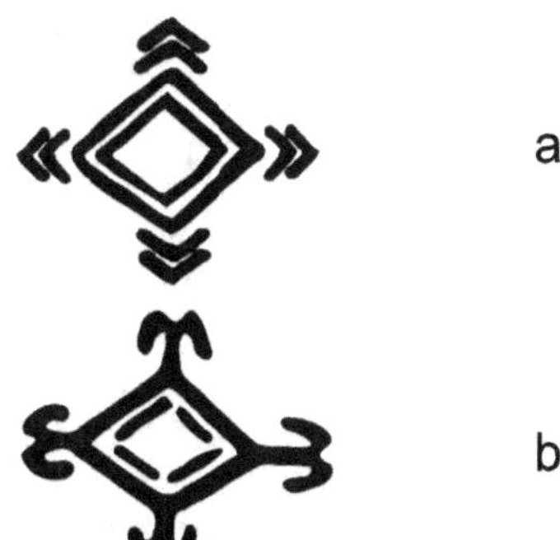

a

b

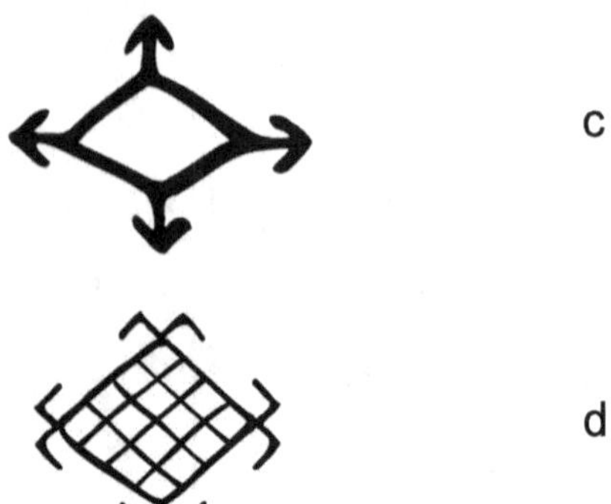

c

d

Ocean

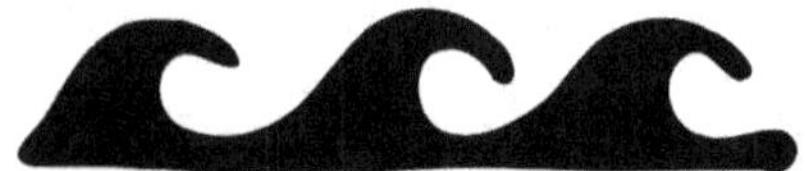

The Ocean is a second home to Polynesian people and the place of rest when they leave for their last voyage (turtles are said to join the departed guiding them to their destination), which means that the sea is sometimes used to represent death, the beyond; since the Ocean is the primary source of food, it's no wonder it impacts so much on traditions, myths and lore. All the creatures living in it are associated to several meanings usually mutuated from their characteristic traits and habits.

The ocean, the sea, can be represented by waves, a few stylizations of which are shown next; they represent **life**, **change** and **continuity**

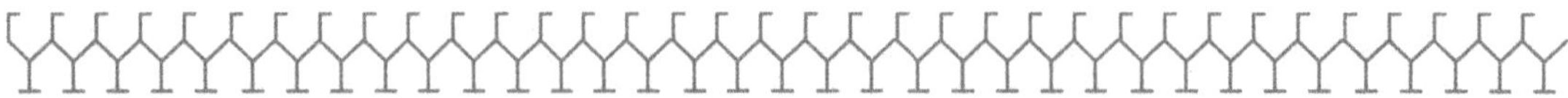

through change, richness.

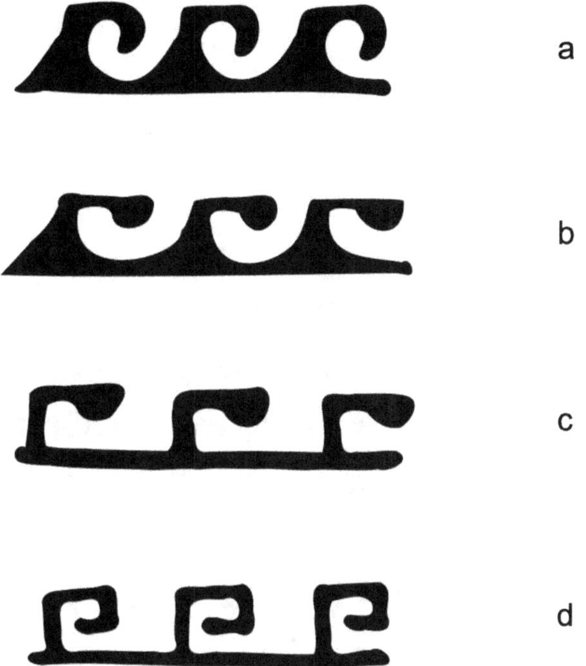

a

b

c

d

Waves can also be used to represent **the world beyond**, the place where the departed go and rest on their last voyage and our **ancestral home** too.

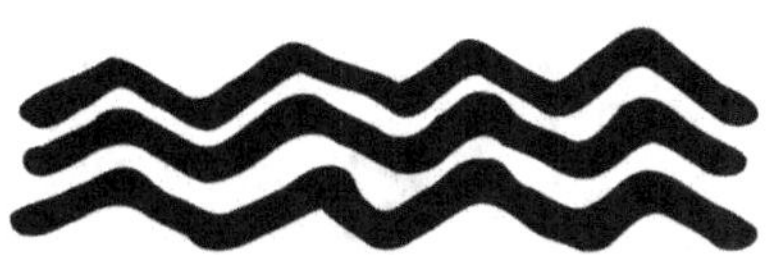

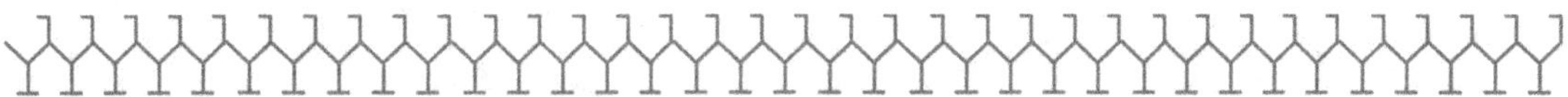

Sun

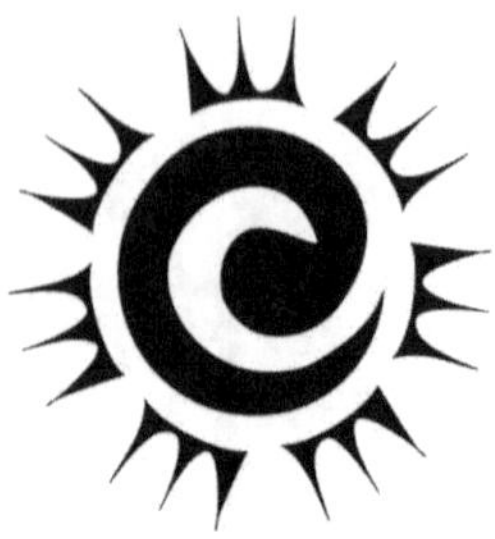

The sun embodies the life giving source, the male energy and it symbolizes **prosperity**, **bright spirit**, **leadership** and **greatness**.

As for many cultures around the world, the cyclic rising and setting of the sun generated the concept of continuous return, of **eternity**, which finds a parallel in the spiral motif.

The rising of the sun is associated to **renewal** and even the sunset is not seen as death, but as a passage to the world beyond.

Depending on which symbols are used to represent the edge of the sun, different meanings get associated together.

Several symbols are fit to create the sun rays, such as the one above, usually representing mountains and symbolizing stability, or like the shark teeth below:

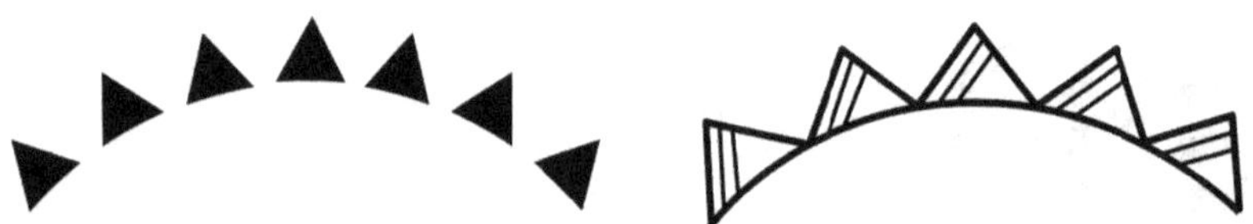

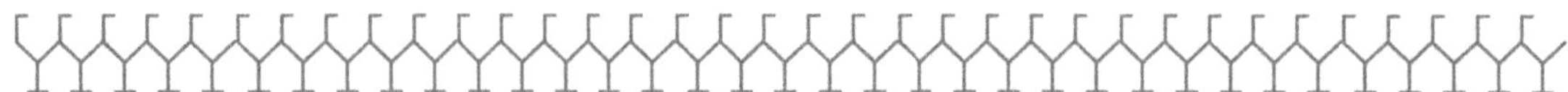

The stylized motif of the honu shell can be used as well and waves are often used too:

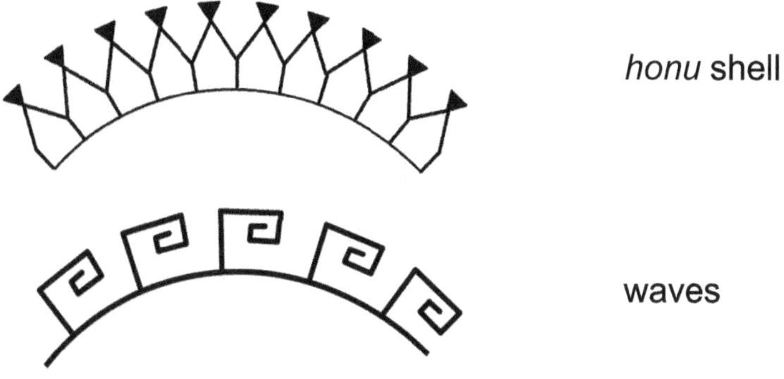

honu shell

waves

Marquesan cross

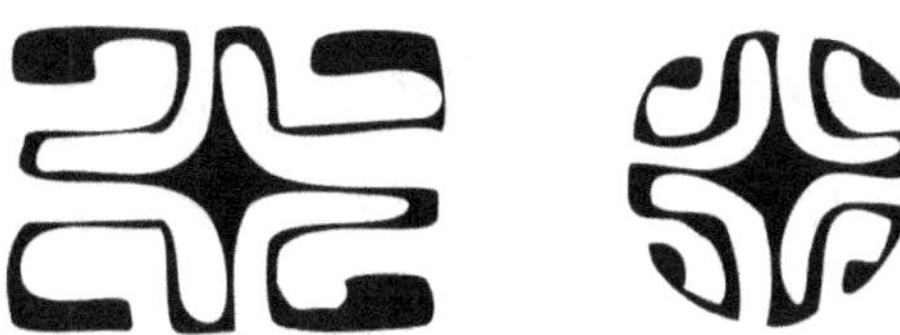

Originally the Marquesan cross seems to have been associated to the turtle shell. It resembles the hindu symbol of sun and has similar meanings, ranging from **eternity** to **harmony** and **balance between the elements**.

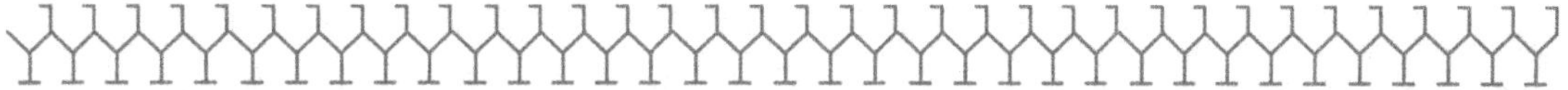

Sea shells

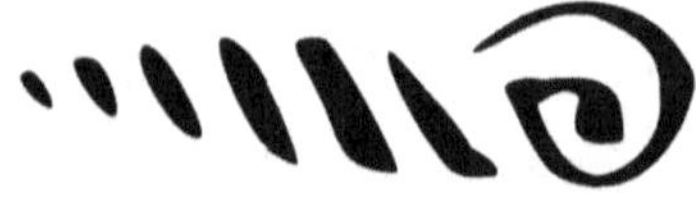

Sea shells played an important role in the life of Polynesian people: their mollusks provided food to them and their shells were used to produce several artifacts for the life of everyday; polished sea shells were also used as money and carved shells were appreciated gifts.

Due to their shape they also symbolize **safe shelter** and **intimacy.**

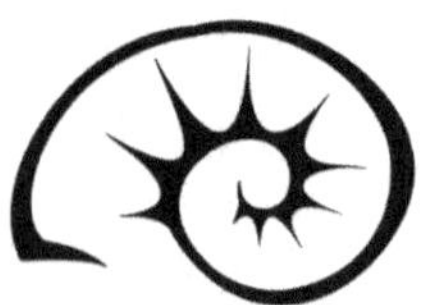 

Bivalve shells such as tridacnas symbolize **couples**, **marriage**, **union**. They are named *api*, which is the root of many words like *apipi* = "joined" or *apipiti* = "together".

They are also used to represent women.

Divinities and spirits

Tiki

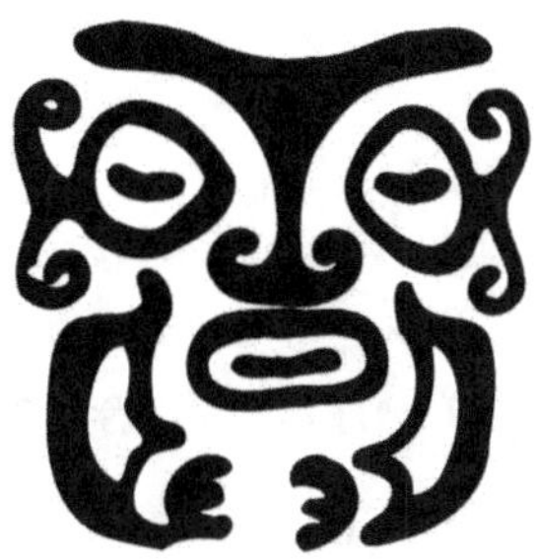

One meaning of the word *tiki* is "figure" and *tiki* is the name given to human-like figures that usually represent semi-gods, as opposed to the *atua*, gods, who usually appear to men under the shape of animals such as lizards.

Like *aumakua*, *tiki* can also represent **deified ancestors**, priests and chiefs who surged to the state of semi-gods after their death.

They symbolize **protection**, **fertility** and they serve as **guardians**.

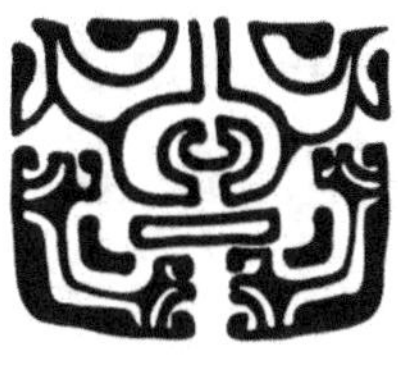

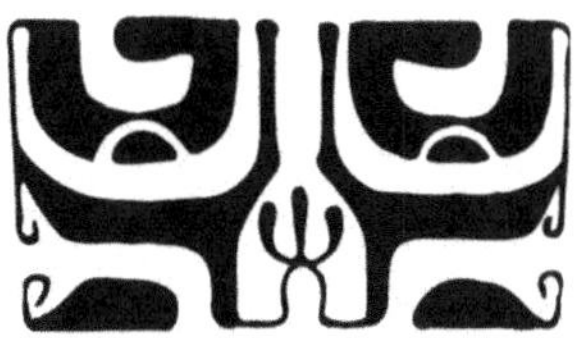

stylizations

By stylizing the *tiki* figure over and over we reach a very simplified version that is called "brilliant eye" where the eyes, nostrils and ears of the *tiki* appear to be the prominent elements:

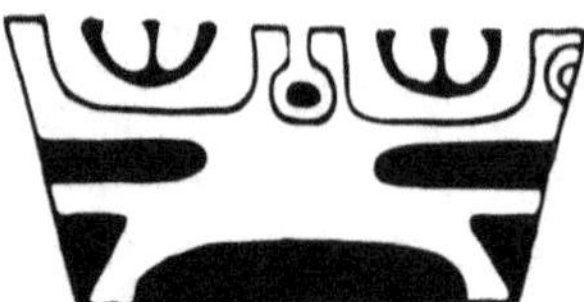

Nostrils remain an important element in the design of *tikis* as they were believed to smell danger before seeing it (this explains why some *tiki* figures have closed eyes).

The all-seeing eye was derived later from the brilliant eye; it was sometimes placed on the back of the knee to scare enemies and ward the back of warriors:

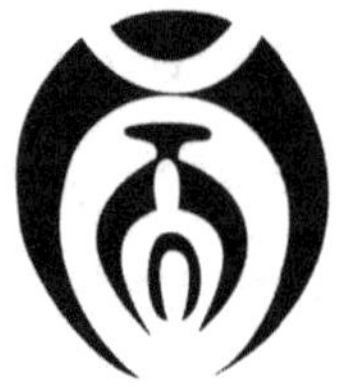

Along the same lines, sometimes only parts of a *tiki* are pictured to bring protection, such as the arms, eyes and hands. In the following samples, the a-b-c series shows how the basic stylized motif is reached:

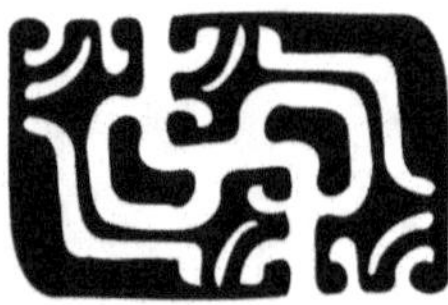   arms

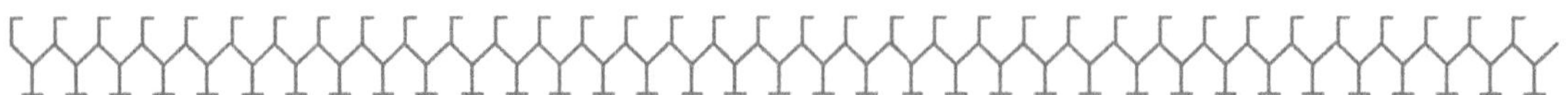

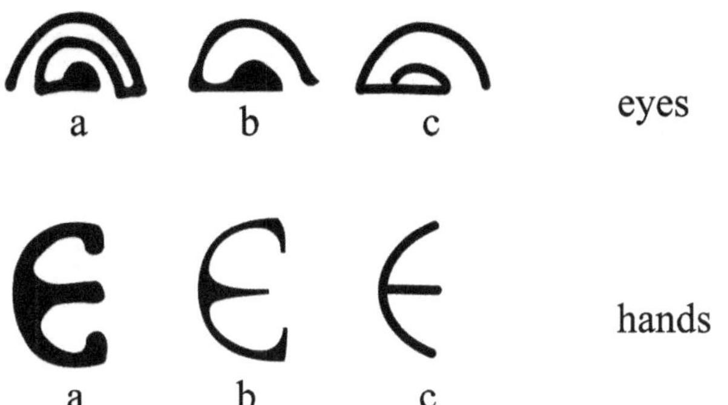

eyes

hands

Tiki figures can be portrayed in front view (sometimes with their tongue stretched out as a symbol of **defiance** to enemies) or side view. In the latter case there are often two *tiki* figures looking in opposite directions, which means that they will bring **protection against dangers coming from all sides**.

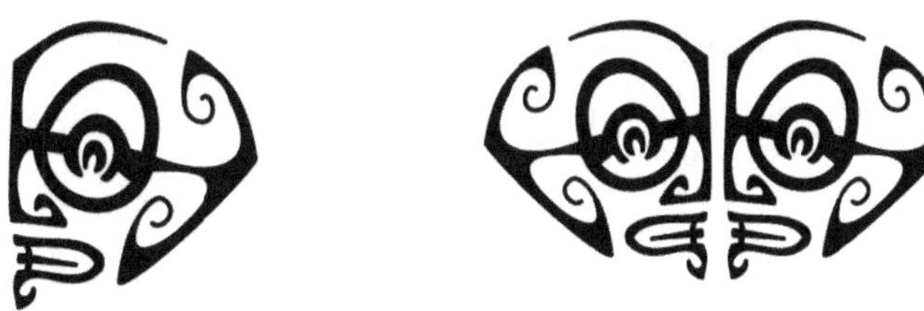

Side view of eyes:

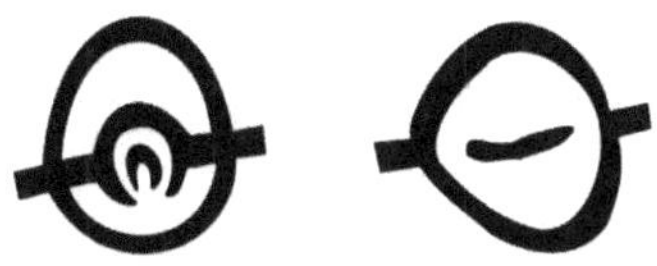

Nostrils:

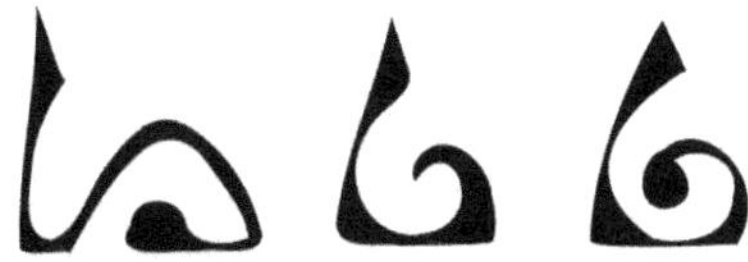

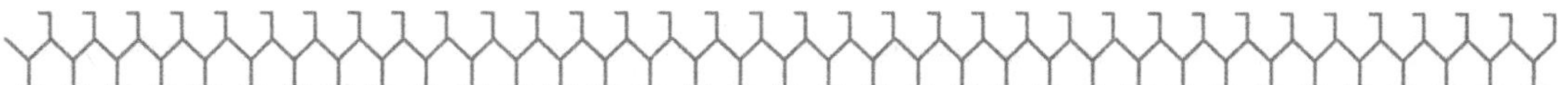

Mouth:

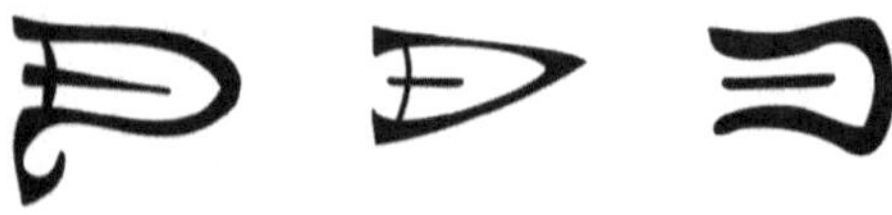

Manaia

The *manaia* is a mythological creature in Maori culture and it is usually depicted with the head of a bird, the body of a man and the tail of a fish, mainly shaped in side view like an eight figure as in the image below. It is considered a **messenger** between the material world and the world of spirits and it symbolizes **protection from evil**, much like a **guardian angel**.

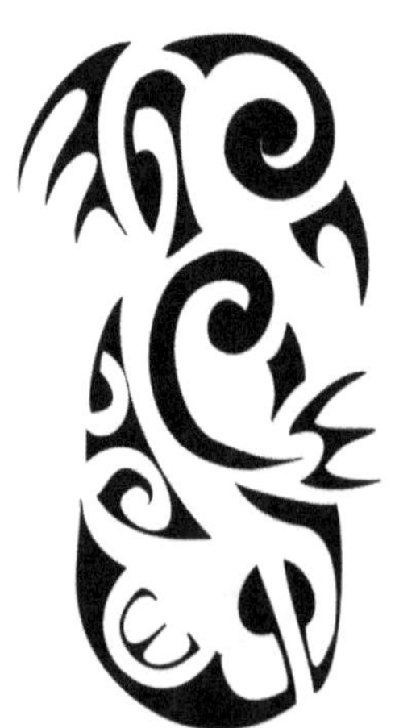

Taniwha

In Maori mythology, *taniwha* are beings living in deep pools of rivers, dark caves, or in the sea, especially where dangerous currents or breakers are present. They have a dual nature and can be either **powerful protective guardians** of people and places (*kaitiaki*), or **dangerous** and predatory beings punishing everyone who does not respect sacred places. As guardians they were also highly valued in war, when they would attack the enemies of their native clan slaying and devouring them. On this account it's not uncommon to see them represented with a spear in a hand and a man in the other hand, in the act of eating him.

They can appear to men under several forms, but they are usually depicted with a human head (with beak-shaped mouth) and the body of a serpent.

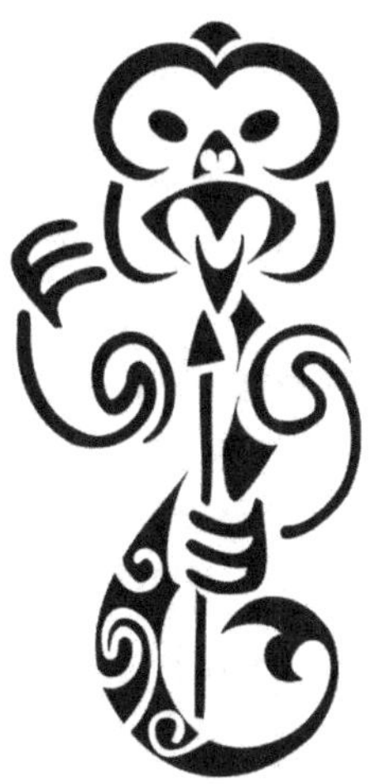

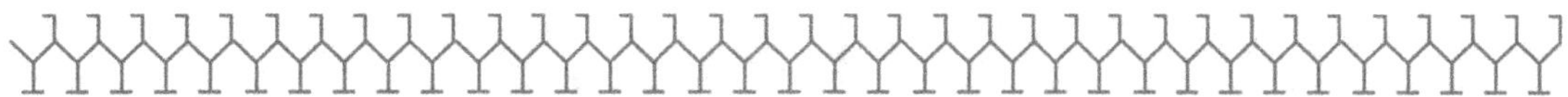

'Aumakua

Aumakua is the name given to **protector spirits** who are related to a family and who are inherited by the family members throughout the generations. They are often **deified ancestors**, famous and respected in life, coming back as guardians for the family, usually showing themselves in the shape of animals to guide, teach, warn and even punish. Mutual respect must exist between people and their *aumakua*.

Flowers and plants

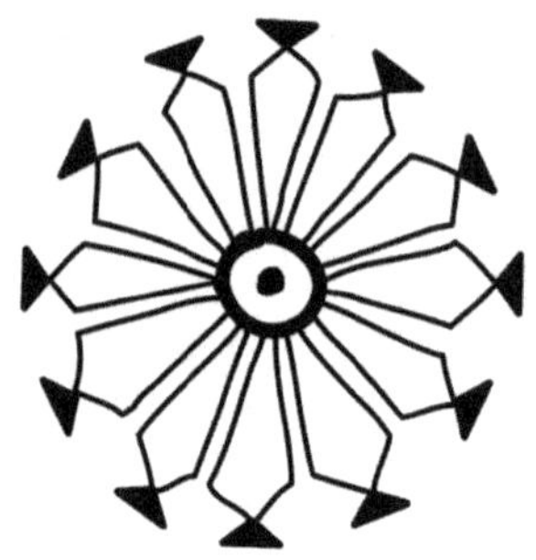

Flowers often appear in Polynesian designs, mainly hibiscus flowers, frangipani and tiare. They usually represent **beauty, femininity** and **joy**, but they also represent **new bloomings, children**. Mostly used by women, they can be worn by men too if they have not bloomed yet.

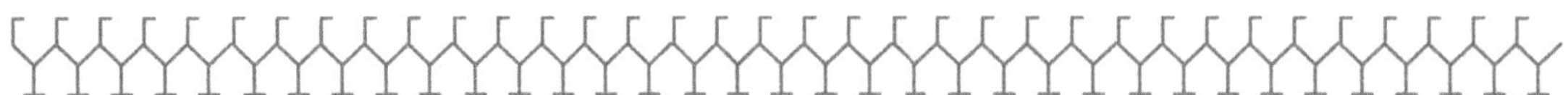

Hibiscus

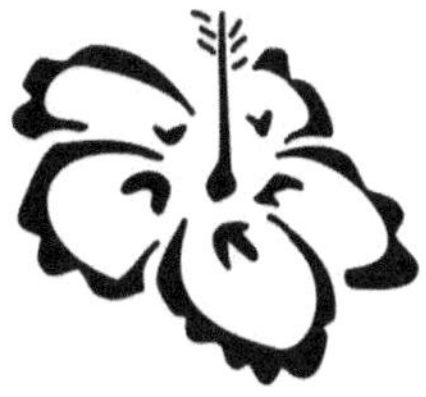

The flower of hibiscus is probably the most renowned flower from the Pacific area. It's the symbol of Hawaii and it symbolizes **beauty**, **femininity**, **passion**. It's also a symbol of the "island vibe", the relaxed and easy-going way of living that is so natural on such naturally blessed islands.

Tiare

The flower of tiare is the national flower of French Polynesia and it has become a symbol to represent traditional Tahitian dance. It symbolizes **beauty**, **grace**, **sensuality**. Tiare flowers are often used to prepare the typical garlands worn around the neck and gifted to visitors, called *ei* or *lei* in Hawaii. Tiare flowers are also worn behind the ear as a hair adornment and in many Polynesian traditions this means that a woman is taken if the flower is placed on the left, available if placed on the right.

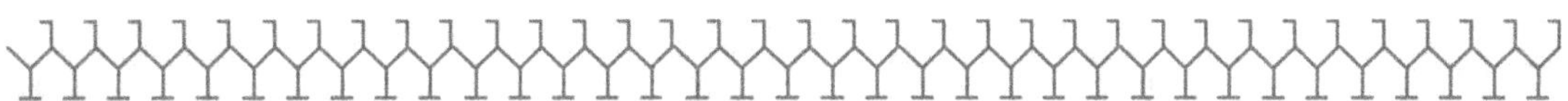

Frangipani

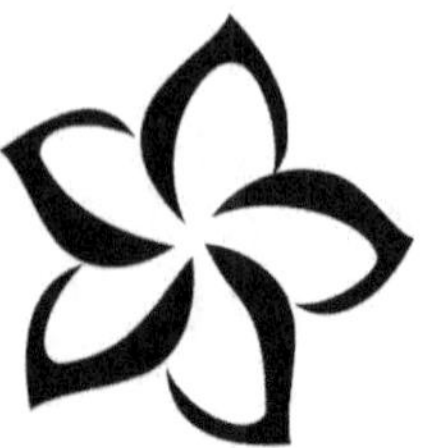

Frangipani flowers (plumerias) share similar meanings with the tiare flowers and they symbolize **beauty, love**.

They can be used to represent **children** and they symbolize **shelter** and **protection** too.

Kava

Kava was a sacred plant, often used in religious ceremonies. A drink was obtained by chewing or pounding its roots, which had lightly intoxicating properties. This drink was used to prepare the mind to **communicate with the *atua***, the gods, or to treat several illnesses. It symbolizes **blessing, healing** and **peace**.

Puawananga flower

Puawananga plants (clematis) were used for treating some illnesses as migraines and thus the flowers of puawananga symbolize **healing**.

Koru

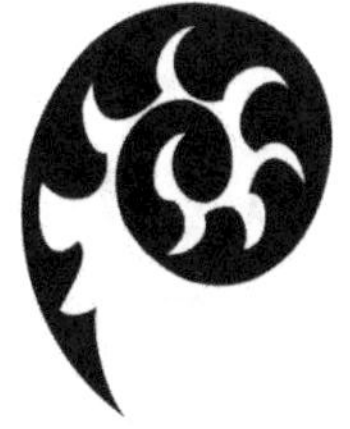

The word *koru* means "fold, loop" and it is used to identify the pattern of the unfolding fern frond. It is a very important element in Maori art and culture and can be found both as a partly rolled line and as a full spiral.

It represents **life**, **new beginnings**. Maori people say: "*Mate atu he tetekura, ara mai he tetekura*", which means "As one fern frond dies, one fern frond is born"; it symbolizes the **continuity of life**, **traditions** and **genealogy**. It's interesting to note that *tete kura* can also be translated as "chief". This is also related to the adult fern,

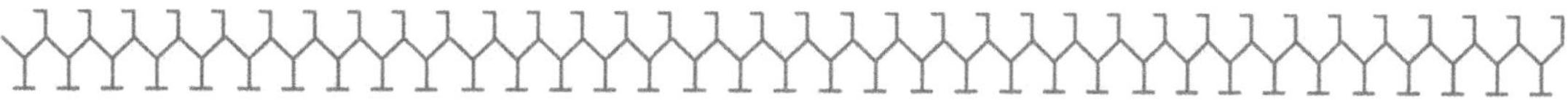

symbolizing **maturity**.

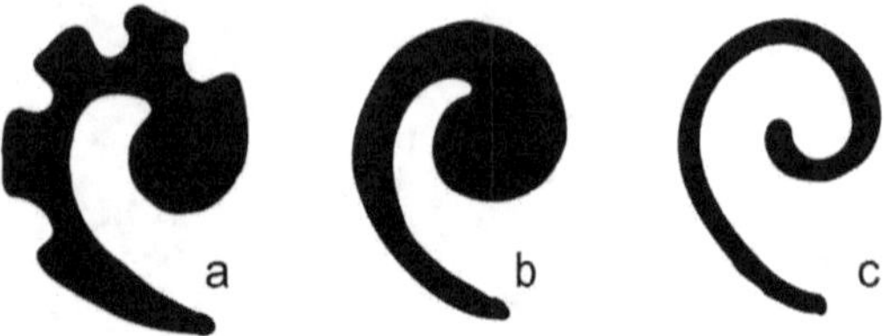

A double *koru* like the one below represents **continuity** and is particularly fit for representing **children, descent**.

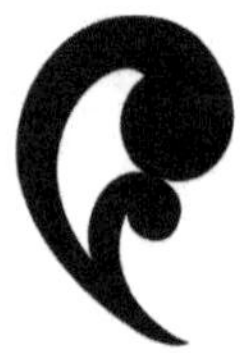

Paired *koru* get stylized to become a double spiral, which is also used in *Tā Moko* tattooing to represent the **ancestors** and to represent a warrior's **genealogy**. Usually spirals are related to female ancestors and double spirals to male ones.

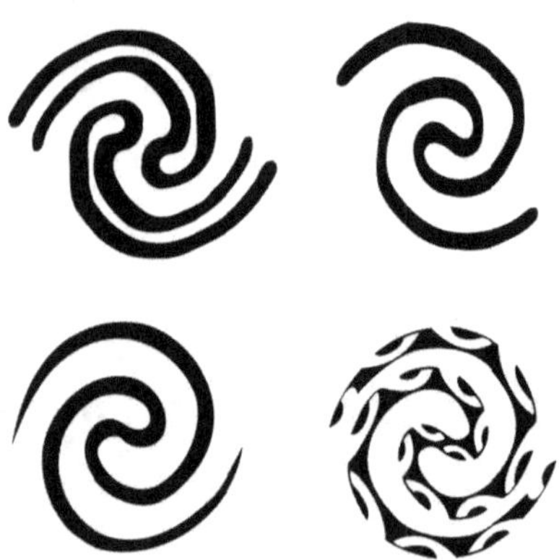

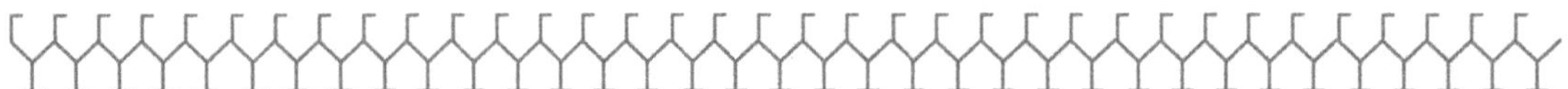

Ipu

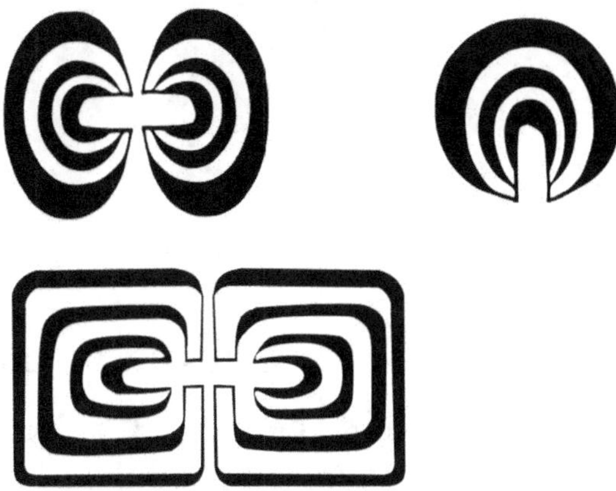

The *ipu* is a stylization of a gourd and it is to Marquesan tattooing what the double spiral is to Maori traditions.

Marquesans used to tattoo their genealogy on the back of the arms, using paired *ipu* placed in a line that featured ancestors and relatives, with the closest ones (or the oldest ones according to some sources) being on top.

It is a very common symbol, appearing in most tattoos and it has many associated meanings, all related to life and its generating force: it's a symbol of **fertility** and **birth** and it is used to represent the mother too.

Two coupled *ipu* usually represent **marriage** much like the coupled *enata* do.

A legend says that Hilo (a sailor and deity) kept the good winds in a gourd and traditions associate the shape of the gourd to the body of Rongo, god of cultivated plants and fertility.

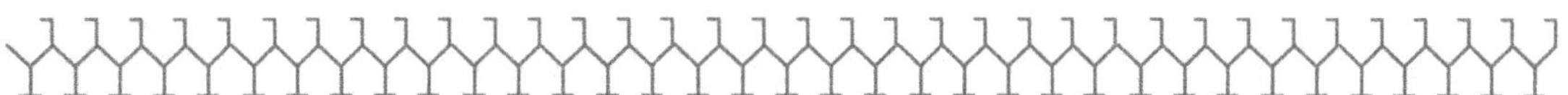

Flax leaves

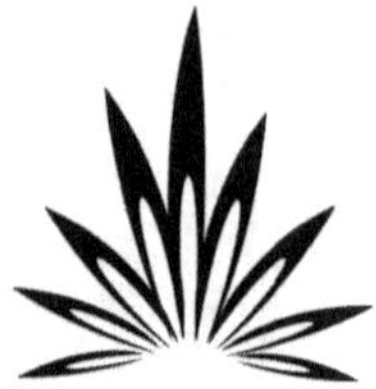

Maori people hold the flax plant sacred as its core represents to them the link between the plant itself, earth and people. Its leaves represent **family**. The inner, smaller leaf, represents the child, with his two parents embracing him from the two sides and ancestors embracing and protecting them all externally like *aumakua* do with family members. When flax leaves were cut, this was always made with great respect, cutting only the outer leaves not to weaken the plant.

The stylized flax leaves motif is called *ritorito*:

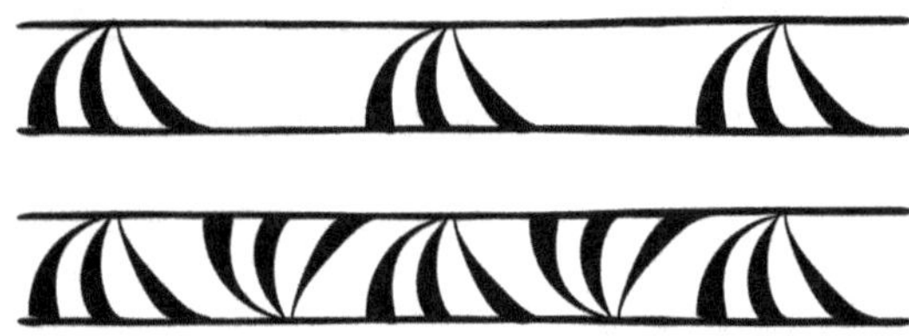

ritorito patterns

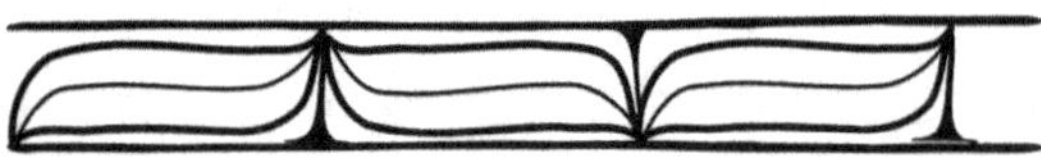

Ti leaves

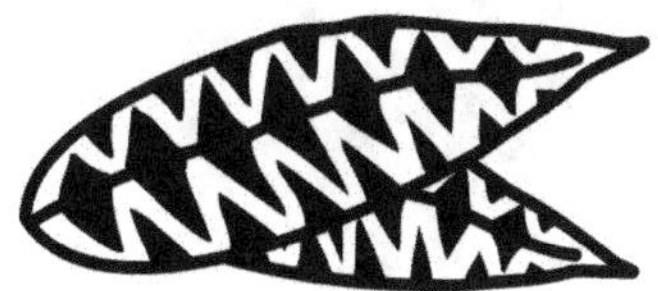

Ti plants were planted at the four corners of the house for **protection**. Their primary meaning is **blessing**.

Braid and cord

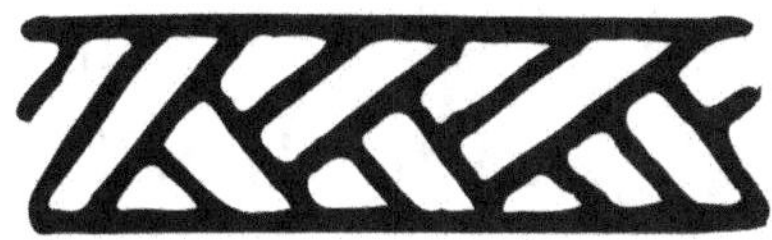

Braids and cords too represent **ancestry**, **union**, having their fibers woven together like the relations between relatives. As the braid is much stronger than the single fiber, a **community** is much stronger than its single elements and the more fibers are joined together, the stronger the cord will be. It also represents **family** and **traditions**: ancestors are the beginning of the cord of a family, with the other end representing the new born babies. The cord will grow longer with new generations, but ancestors will always remain a part of it and they shall maintain their importance for the strength of the rope. We shall not forget our ancestors and traditions or our cord will become smaller and weaker.

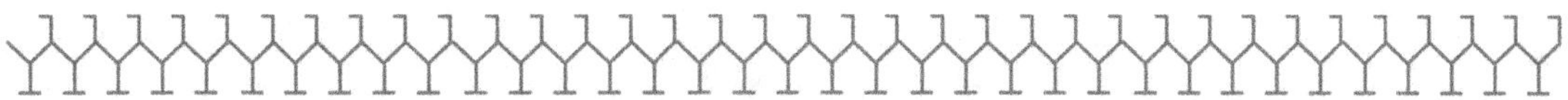

Coconut

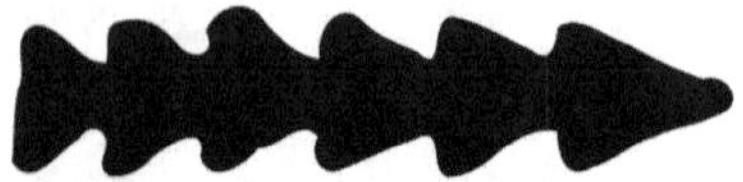

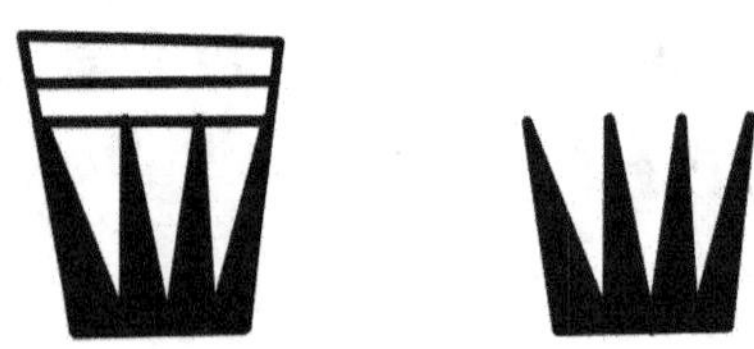

Palm trees are symbolic of the Pacific islands and they represent **peace**, **good vibrations**, **serenity**. Coconut palms are a gift to islanders for they give fibers, fruit, wood, even bowls and they represent **plenty**, **prosperity**.

Other elements

Te ara poutama

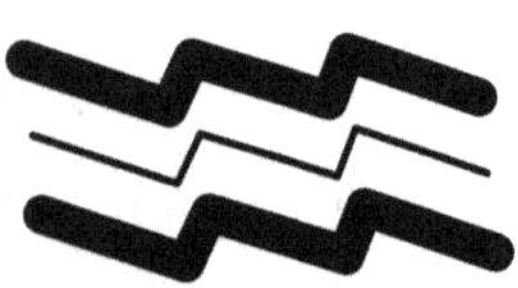

It can be translated as "The ragged path"; this motif represents the **path to knowledge**, which is never straight and easy.

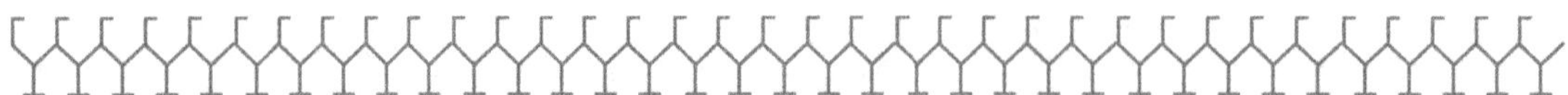

Te ha

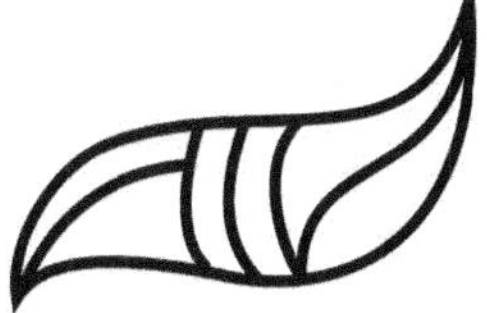

It represents the **breath of life**.

Pito

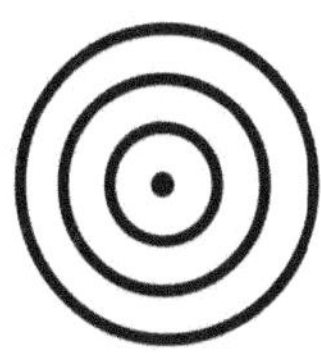

It represents the navel and it symbolizes **birth** and **independence**, from the cut of the umbilical cord.

Twist

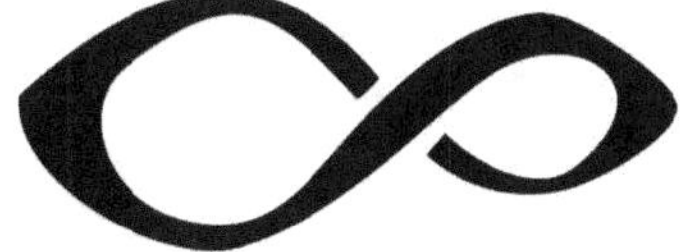 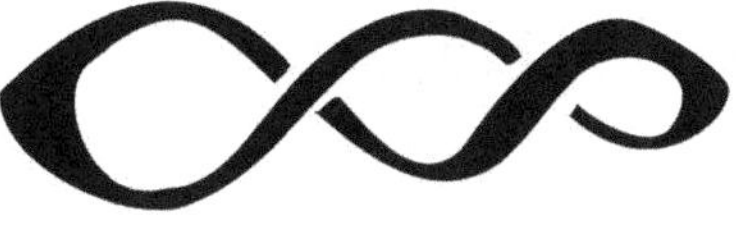

The twist (here horizontal but usually vertical) symbolizes **eternal love** and **union**. It represents two lives that, even if separated at times (e.g for a voyage) will always get back to stay together in the end. The triple twist version is usually referred to the **meeting of different cultures**.

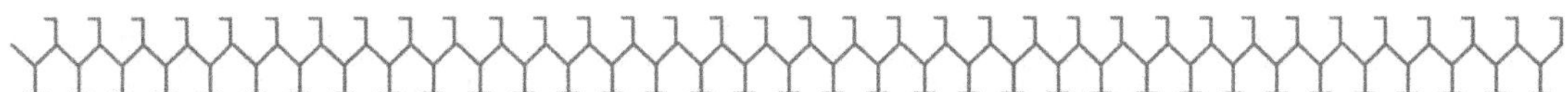

The path of Kamehameha

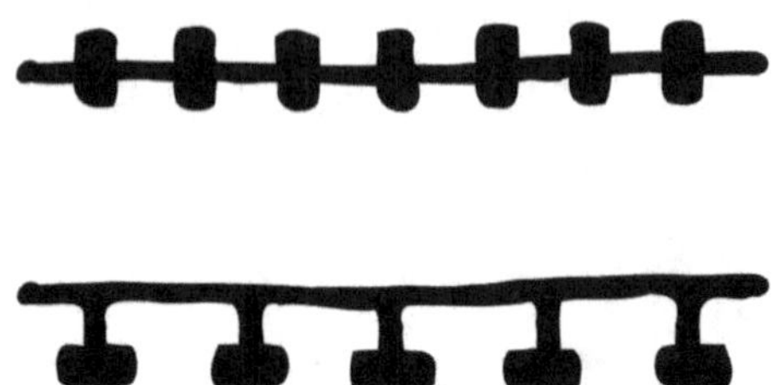

Kamehameha was a renowned Hawaiian chief and this motif called "the path of Kamehameha" is usually used to represent **a trail, a challenging path**.

Standing stones

They represent **achievements**.

Side note:

Traditional designs should not include elements that do not belong to Pacific cultures (strictly traditional ones should actually stick to a single style per design), but there can be many reasons for having different elements included: perhaps you may want to incorporate elements from other cultures because they represent your own background.

Our opinion is: go for it if it's meaningful for you!

Style them in a fashion that integrates finely into your Polynesian design (you may redraw them using native elements) or let them stand out adding an exotic touch to the tattoo.

It will not be offensive to Polynesian cultures as long as it is done in a graceful, respectful way.

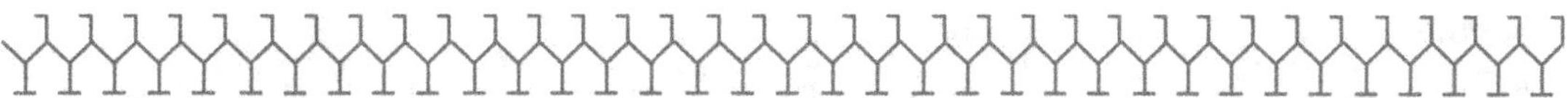

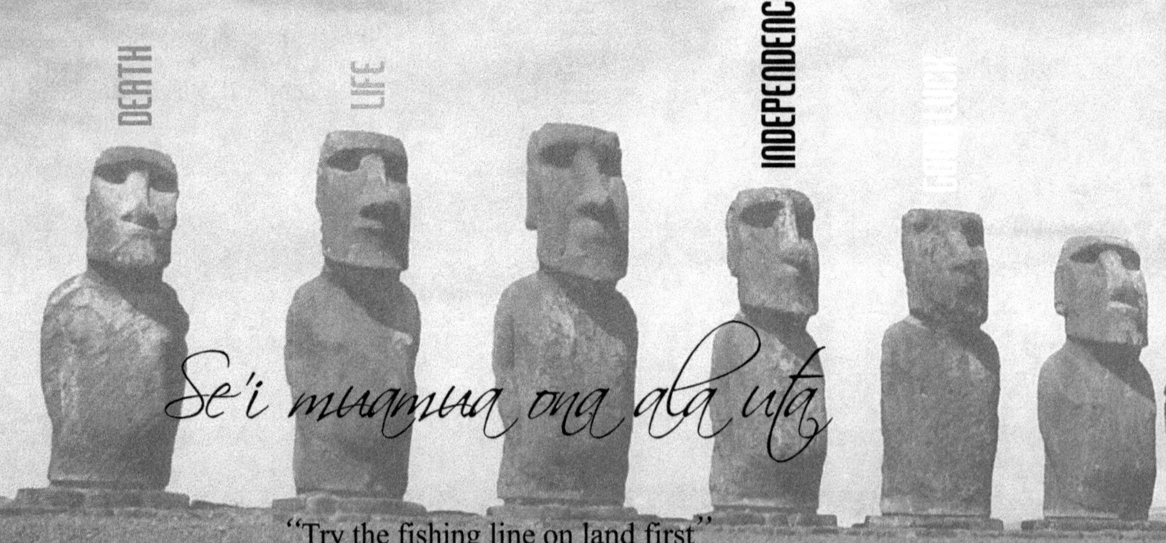

DEATH
LIFE
INDEPENDENCE
Se'i muamua ona ala uta
"Try the fishing line on land first"
"Ponder your actions, don't be impulsive"

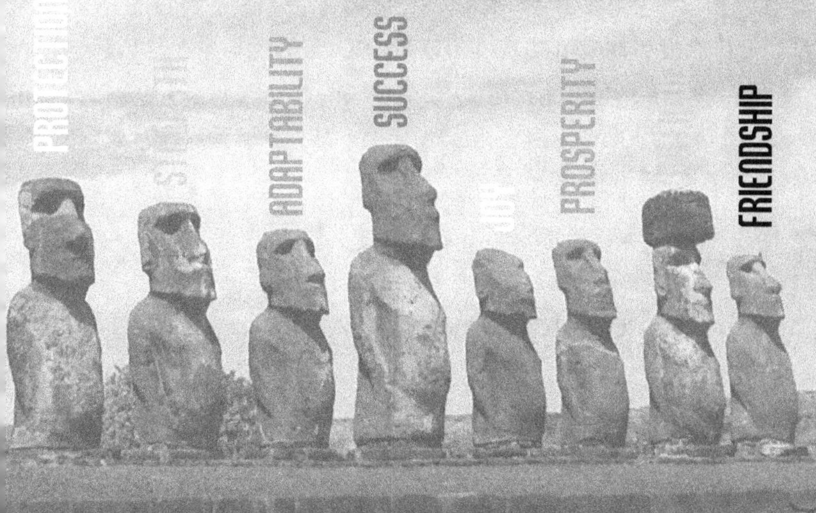
PROTECTION
STRENGTH
ADAPTABILITY
SUCCESS
HOPE
PROSPERITY
FRIENDSHIP

"Se'i muamua ona ala uta"
—Try the fishing line on land first:
Ponder your actions, don't be impulsive.

If you are going to tell your story with a Polynesian tattoo, this chapter will be your faithful travel companion, a "quick and dirty" list of many elements, feelings and qualities you may want to use, the starting point to decide what elements will be the best for your purpose.

There are often several ways and elements that can be used to represent each meaning. We are reporting the main ones, with the most used elements coming first and the secondary ones following in order of importance. The best elements should be chosen based on their meanings and on how well they integrate into the design.

A

abundance: fish hook, net, fish, coconut flowers, whale, waves, bonito

accomplishment: manta, fish hook

adaptability: octopus, shark

adventure: canoe

adversities: eels

affection: sea shell

alertness: seagulls

ancestors: ipu, aumakua, cord

awakening: koru

B

balance: Marquesan cross, manaia, tiki

be prepared: adze, fish hook

beauty: hibiscus, manta, tiare flowers

beyond: waves

birth: koru, ipu

blessing: ti leaves, kava

boldness: spear heads

bonds: braid, ani ata, twist (eternal love), dolphin

bravery: mere, spear heads

bright: sun

brotherhood: sharing one same tattoo, paired pigeons

C

calm: turtle, sun

care: whale, turtle

carefree: butterfly, hibiscus flower

carpe diem: hibiscus flower

to challenge: warrior mask or tiki with outstretched tongue

change: waves

chief: mere, fish hook

children: flowers

committment: checkered bracelet

communication: lizard (to the gods)

community: birds (when many together), flying fox, ani ata

consciousness: sun, navel

continuity: koru (of life), waves (through change)

couple: coupled enata, bivalve shell, coupled ipu

courage: mere, spear heads

craftmanship: adze, gecko

creativity: adze

D

danger: eel

death: waves (usually backwards)

dedication: name (there is no Polynesian alphabet: check our appendix on maorigrams for this)

defiance: warrior mask or tiki with outstrecthed tongue

departed: ani ata, turtle with enata

descent: double koru, ipu, double spiral and spiral

determination: hammerhead shark, centipede

devotion: tiki, frangipani

disease: moray eel

discovery: frigate bird, sea turtle

disguise: ray (especially of emotions)

disposability: canoe, fish hook

divination: lizard

E

earth: mountains, flax

elegance: manta

elements (balance of): Marquesan cross, manaia

energy: sun, bonito tail, ray

eternal life: Marquesan cross

eternity: sun, spiral, Marquesan cross

evil spirit: eel

extra-sensorial perception: gecko, lizard

F

faith: net, cord

family: sea turtle, flax leaves, braid, cord

father: tiki

fertility: tiki, ipu, koru, turtle

fighting spirit: centipede, spear heads, barracuda, hammerhead shark

fire: birds

foundation: turtle

force: adze (physical and moral)

flying: birds, manta

freedom: birds, manta, butterfly

friendship: dolphin

fruitful: flowers

G

genealogy: coupled ipu

generosity: net, canoe

goals: dots, "fixed points", marlin (reaching the goals)

gods: tiki, lizard, aumakua

good vibrations: hibiscus flower, manta, palm trees, sun

grace: tiare flower

greatness: mere, sun, fish hook, ani ata

growth: koru

guardian: tiki, manaia, taniwha, aumakua

guidance: stars, tiki, shark

guile: shark

H

happiness: sun, flowers

harmony: Marquesan cross, manaia, waves

healing: puawananga flower, kava, octopus, Marquesan cross

health: gecko, lizard

heaven: ani ata

help: two birds chasing each other, net

hero: kena

hidden treasure: sea shell

higher perspective: birds

honesty: mere, fish hook

honor: mere

hope: sun

hyperactivity: flying fox

I

illness: eel

independence: navel

intelligence: fish hook

intimacy: sea shell

island vibe: hibiscus flower, palm trees

J

join: braid, cord

joy: dolphin, sun, flowers

justice: mere

K

kindness: tiare flower

knowledge: adze, fish hook, dolphin

L

land: mountains

leadership: sun

lethal: orca

life: koru, sun, lizard

life and death cycle: Marquesan cross

light through darkness: sea urchin

longevity: turtle

love: twist, sea shell, frangipani flowers, ray

loyalty: dog

luck: lizard, sun, fish hook

M

magic: lizard

male: spear heads

man: enata

marriage: coupled enata, checkered pattern, coupled ipu, dolphin

maternal instinct: flying fox, bat, whale

maturity: adult fern frond

meeting: braid, triple twist (meeting of cultures)

money: sea shells (sun for success)

mother: ipu

move forward: canoe

N

navigator: sea turtle, waves

new start, new life: koru

nobility: mere, flying fox

nurturing: whale

O

observation: gecko

only child: pigeon

operosity: flying fox, adze

overcoming obstacles: adze, spear heads

P

passion: hibiscus flower

path: canoe, path of Kamehameha, braid (path of life)

path to knowledge: Te ara pautama

patience: turtle

peace: coconut palm, flowers, kava, mere, sun

people: enata, flax

perceptiveness: gecko

perseverance: bonito, hammerhead shark

playfulness: dolphin, flowers

plenty: waves, fish hook, fish, coconut flowers, sugar cane

positivity: sun, flower

power: sun, barracuda, shark

pride: bird (represented by a different bird among a group of similar ones)

promise: fish hook

prosperity: fish hook, fish, coconut flowers

protection: tiki, manaia, taniwha, aumakua, shark teeth, fish scales, manta, hammerhead shark, orca

purity: frangipani, sun

Q

quick: marlin, bird

R

rebellion: centipede

regeneration: koru, lizard

renewal: unfolding koru, moon

resourcefulness: fish hook

respect: mere, net, waves

responsibilities in the community: canoe

resting place: waves

rise above: bird

rough outside and soft inside: sea urchin

S

safe return: seagull

sailing: bird

sea: waves, manta

search: frigate, net, gecko

sensuality: tiare flower

serenity: palm trees, hibiscus flower

sexuality: sea shell, hibiscus flower, eel

sharp mind: marlin, swordfish

shelter: sea shell, turtle, frangipani

singularity: obtained by inserting a different element among similar ones (see also pride)

skill: fish hook, adze

sky: ani ata, semi-circular motifs

smartness: octopus

sociality: dolphin, flying fox, bat

solidarity: net

speed: marlin, shark

spiritual force: tiki, aumakua

stability: mountains, enata

stability through change: waves

strength: spear heads, adze, hammerhead shark, shark teeth

success: sun, fish hook, bird

supernatural powers: gecko, lizard

survival: lizard

swiftness: orca

T

teaching: adze

teamwork: canoe, braid, net

tenacity: hammerhead shark, centipede

tradition: cord, braid, double koru, ipu

transformation: moon

travel: sea turtle, frigate, waves, canoe

trust: mere

U

unity, union: braid, cord, net, flax (family), twist (love)

universe: ani ata

V

valiance: spear heads

vision: lizard

vital breath: te ha

vitality: sun

victorious: sun, mere

voyage: frigate, sea turtle (by sea)

W

warrior: spear heads, kena, centipede

water: waves

wealth: fish hook

wind: ipu, Marquesan cross

wisdom: dolphin, whale

woman: ipu, bivalve shells

X - Y

Z

zeal: stone adze

A'ohe hana nui ka alu'ia

"No task is too big when done together"

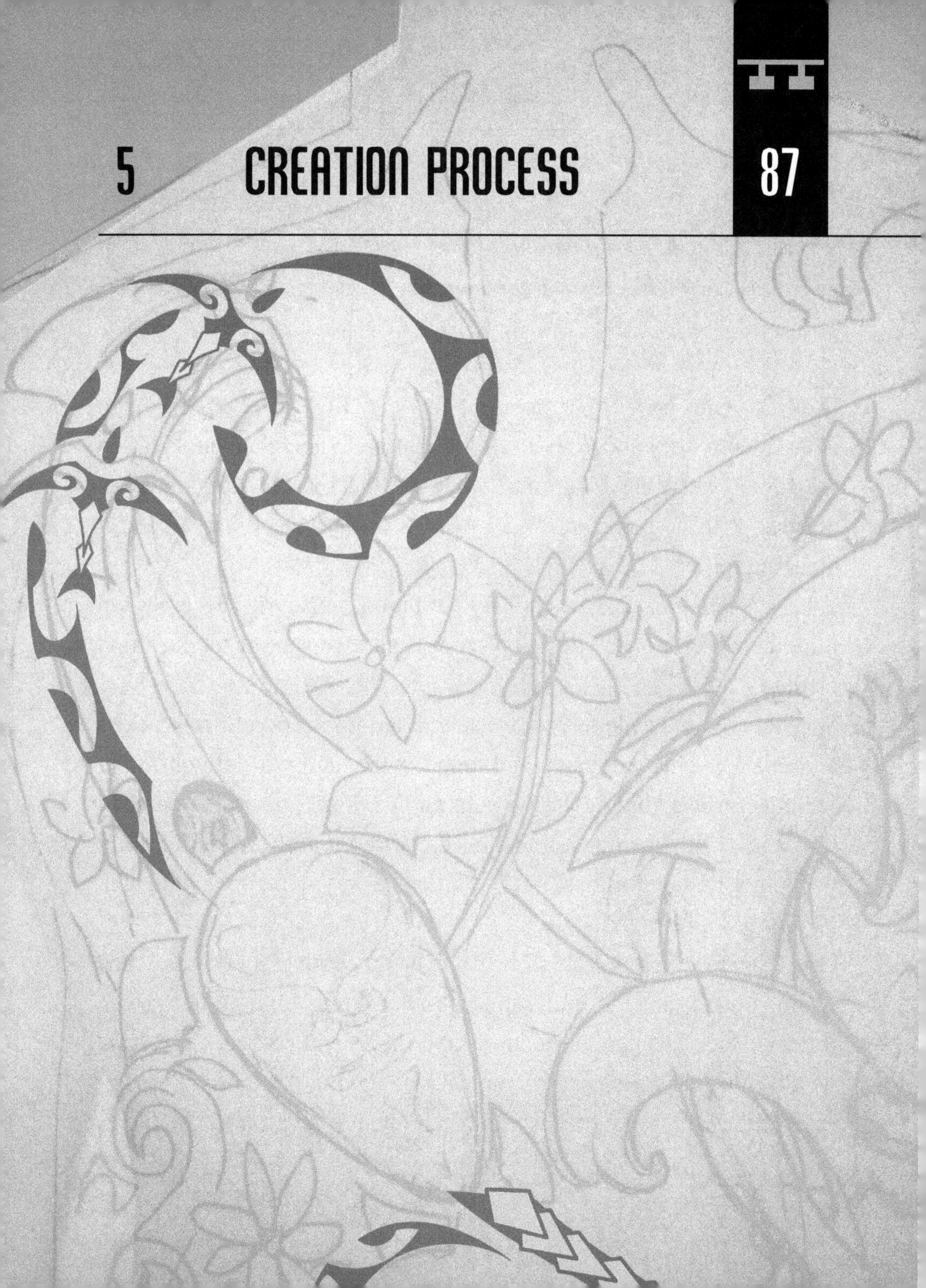

"A'ohe hana nui ka alu'ia"
—No task is too big when done together

Tattoos can be very important in the life of everyone and consequently they should be well thought of. When choosing a tattoo we should keep clear in mind what are the reasons that made us decide for it, be them purely aestethical or because it has a special meaning for us.

When creating a Polynesian styled tattoo, meaning becomes an important aspect of the decision process and we should set our mind forth to it.

Whenever you decide to prepare such a tattoo, keep your mind calm and relaxed. This will carry bad moods away and will let your inner feelings surface guiding you in your choice. Focus on what you want to express and let your tattoo find the way through to you: usually we do not find our tattoos, but our tattoos always find a way to reach us if only we learn to listen.

Don't set for such a task if you are in the wrong mood, or when feelings such as rage and sadness are guiding you. A tattoo can influence our feelings, our actions and in the end our way of living: would you like to keep a memo on you saying "sadness, despair" every time you look at it, or would you better have one that always tells you "hope, be strong"?

One last tip: take your time. Your tattoo will last your whole life; what are a few days or a few months when you are creating something virtually eternal for you? Keep changing it if you are not 100% satisfied: when you find the right design, you will know!

A Samoan tattooing chant (chants sung while a tattoo is being tapped) says:

E isia le 'ula, isia le fau,
'A e le isia siau tatau,
'O siau 'ula tutumau,
E te alu ma 'oe i le tu'ugamau.

The necklace breaks, the cord breaks,
But your tattoo does not break into pieces,
This necklace is forever,
And goes with you to the grave.

After you are sure about the meanings and the position, you may have a look at the quick reference from the previous chapter to identify the elements that will help you convey the right meanings. List them down and check the chapter on symbolism to select the ones that fit your ideas best (remember that there are usually several elements available to represent the same concept).

The choice of the right elements is also influenced by the size you have to fit in: bigger sizes will allow for a wider choice whilst smaller sizes will probably require more stylized elements to be used.

Once you have the meanings and the elements, you have to find how to integrate the elements meaningfully. Reorder your list by importance: the most important elements will be bigger or will be central in your design and minor elements will be used to complete the design. If you want to tell a story, elements will be laid down sequentially, linked in a flow where every aspect is related to the next one as in a chain.

A well structured design should follow and enhance the lines of the body, flowing along the muscles and not breaking them. Round elements are best suited for joints such as ankles and upper shoulders; longer elements will work best for arms and legs; triangular shapes fit nicely on the upper and lower back, groin and collar bone to name a few examples.

Samoan sleeve tattoos are perfect to show how following anatomy can help making outstanding designs:

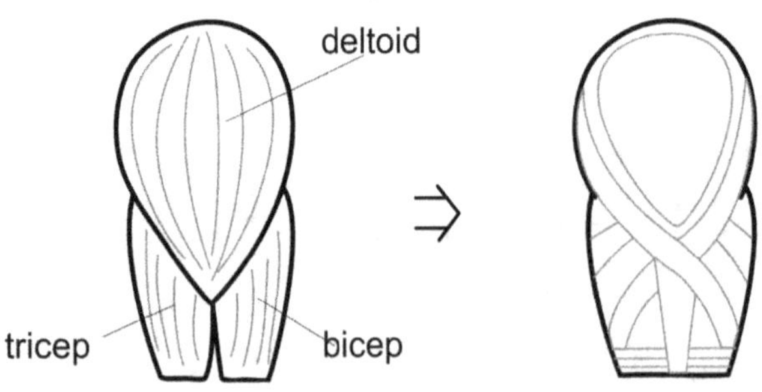

Virtually any design can be adapted to follow the lines of the body, perhaps integrating it with other patterns sharing the same meaning:

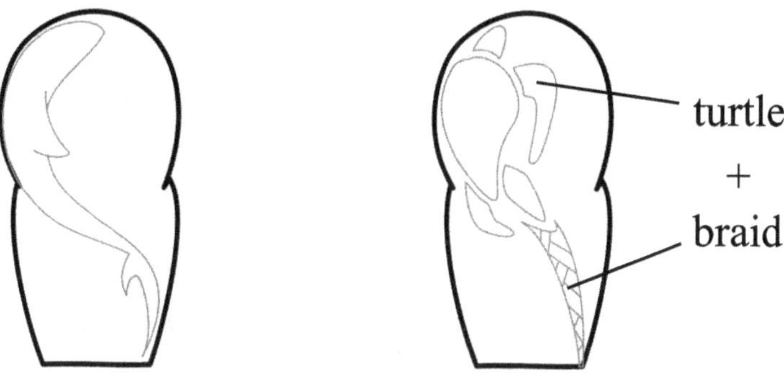

If you have the chance to, take a picture of the area to be tattooed and use it as a canvas for your sketches; print several copies of it so that you can try several solutions and compare them to see which one you like the most. Start laying down the elements by using simple outlines: what is important now is not to make a beautiful design (that will be the final result) but to make a very simple draft where all the elements fit and find their natural placement.

If you don't feel comfortable with freehand sketching, just keep the image on your computer, surf the Internet and search for photos of the animals you want to include in your design, possibly in the same position you want (e.g. a swimming turtle, top view), resize and position them on your photo.

Not a computer guy? Print them all and do some patchworking! Those will be your guidelines.

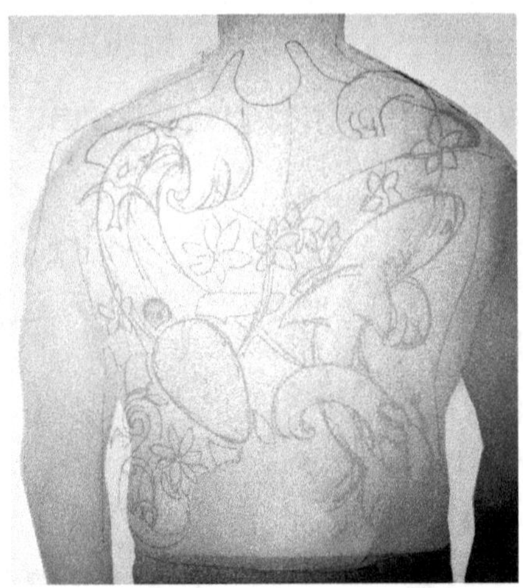

Do not worry if it doesn't look perfect from the start: take your time to digest it, understand what looks or feels wrong and change it. The more you do this, the more the whole process will become natural and fast.

After completing the design you can start replacing the roughly sketched elements with the corresponding Polynesian symbols:

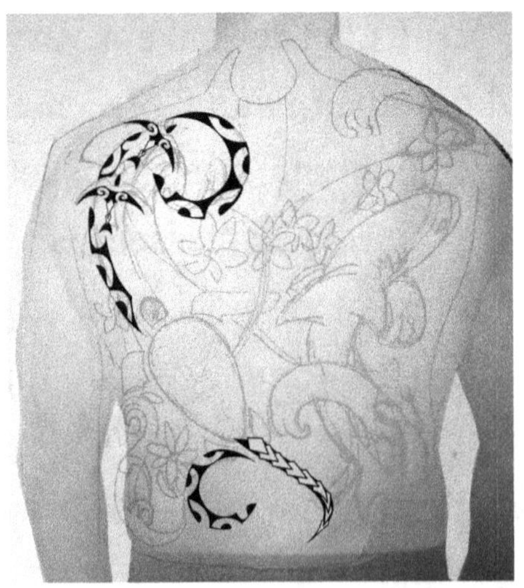

In general, male designs will have thicker outlines and elements and feminine ones will have smaller elements with thin outlines and larger blank spaces among the elements.

As a side note, at least 1.5 mm should separate the various black elements so that the design will not degrade to a black spot over time. Since colours are usually not present in traditional tribal tattooing, blank spaces have almost the same importance of black areas: they can draw the eye towards specific elements and they can contribute to adding meanings to the whole design (just think of the blank *koru*-shaped elements in Maori tattoos).

Case studies

We will analyze here a few designs in detail to see how they were structured, to get an idea of the design process behind the curtains.

Please, do not copy these designs: they tell the story of someone who is not you ... they are meant to give an insight on the creation process to help you design yours!

- Jakub's armbands

- Domiziano's short sleeve

- Poulomi's half sleeve

- Michelle's ankle tattoo

Jakub's armbands

Jakub requested two armbands to represent the union between him and his wife Anna with their names inside the design:

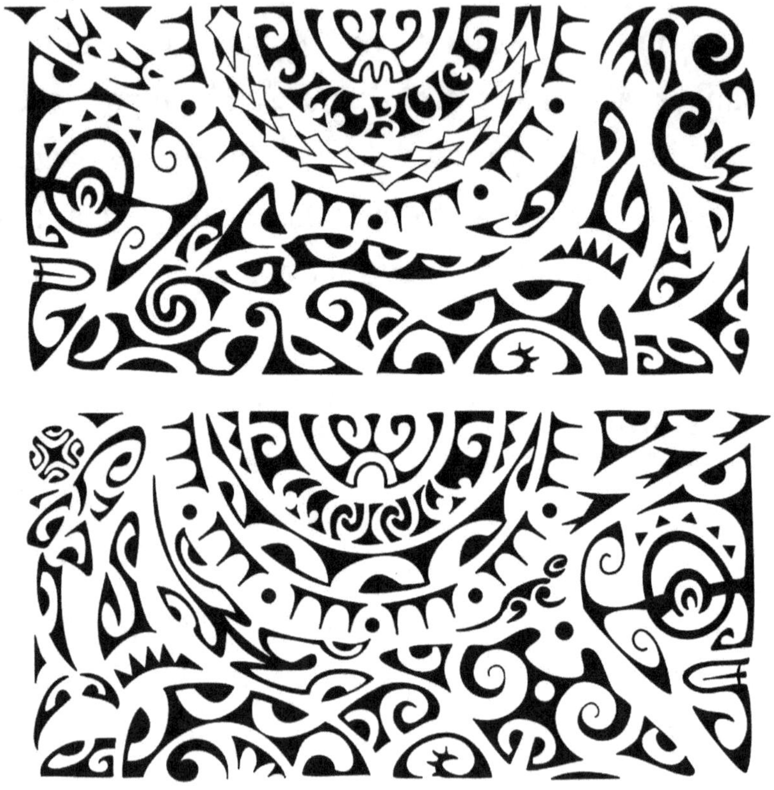

Requested meanings and elements:

Wedding, union, love, protection, strength, turtle, sun, shark, fish hook, lizard, manta, waves, gecko, hammerhead shark, Jakub and Anna names.

step 1: deciding the appropriate elements

Enata: man and woman

Turtle: family

Double spiral: union

Sun: eternity, positivity, joy

Sea shells: love, intimacy

Tiki: protection

Spear heads: strength, warrior

Moon: femininity, fertility

Hammerhead shark: determination, tenacity

Manta: beauty, elegance

Shark: adaptability

Fish and fish hook: plenty, prosperity

Lizard: luck

Gecko: health

Waves: change

Koru: new life

Mountains: stability

Islands: goals, the place to be reached

Chasing birds: help to the dear ones

Marquesan cross: harmony, balance

Maorigrams for the names

Checking the quick reference can help you speed up the process.

step 2: deciding how to dispose them

We have two separate armbands that shall represent union, the creation of a family through the wedding of two people. Each armband will then represent one of them and some elements will be shared.

We kept the right arm (stronger) for him and the left one (closer to the heart) for his wife: the human figure in the center of his one represents him, the man, surrounded by a maorigram of his name Jakub (see appendix for more on maorigrams) and by spear heads (the warrior, strength, courage), with a sun around it (eternity, positivity) made of mountains and islands (stability and the place to be reached); his wife's one features a female figure surrounded by a maorigram of her name Anna, with a moon of waves (femininity, fertility) instead of the spear heads, surrounded by the sun:

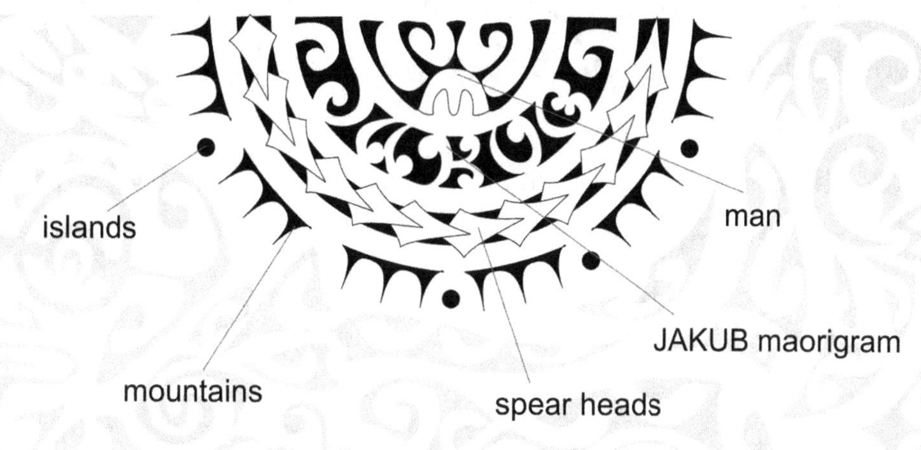

islands
man
mountains
spear heads
JAKUB maorigram

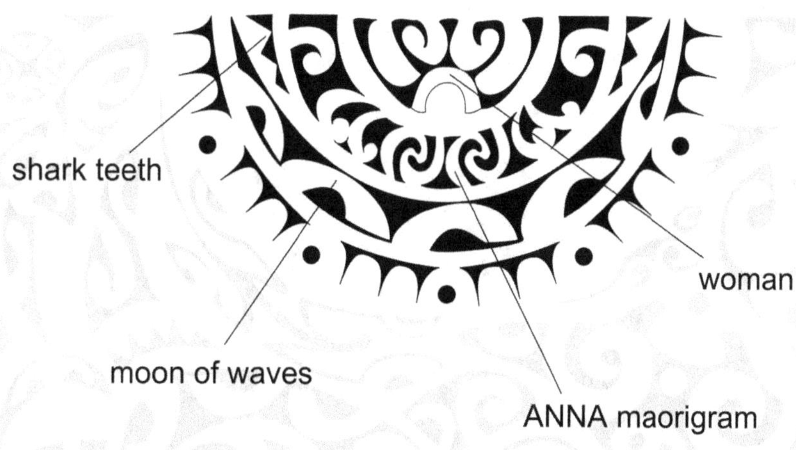

shark teeth
woman
moon of waves
ANNA maorigram

A turtle was chosen to represent family. The same turtle was split to be part of both designs, pointing to the front of the arms to symbolize it will last in the future.

The front flippers of the turtle are made of fish hooks to bring prosperity to the family.

Anna's turtle has a *koru* inside to symbolize she will one day carry new life.

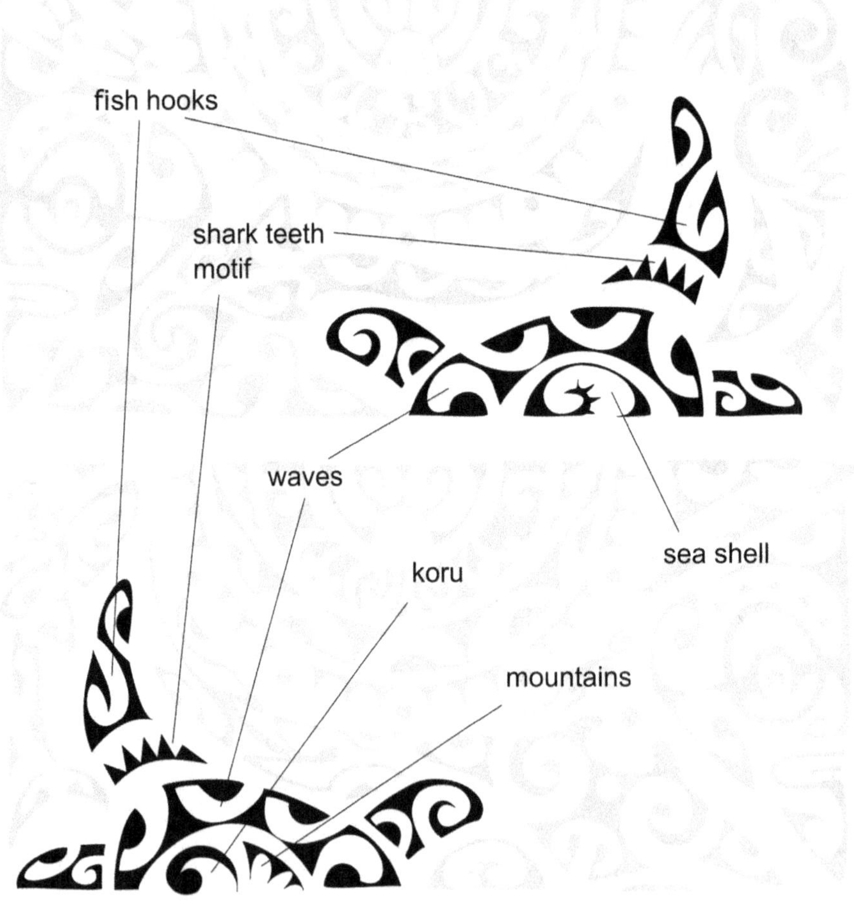

There are half a sun and half a turtle on each armband to symbolize that joy and family are only half if Jakub and Anna are separate and become complete when they are together.

Both the armbands have the same sea shell (love, intimacy) and protective *tiki* figures watch them both, one on each side:

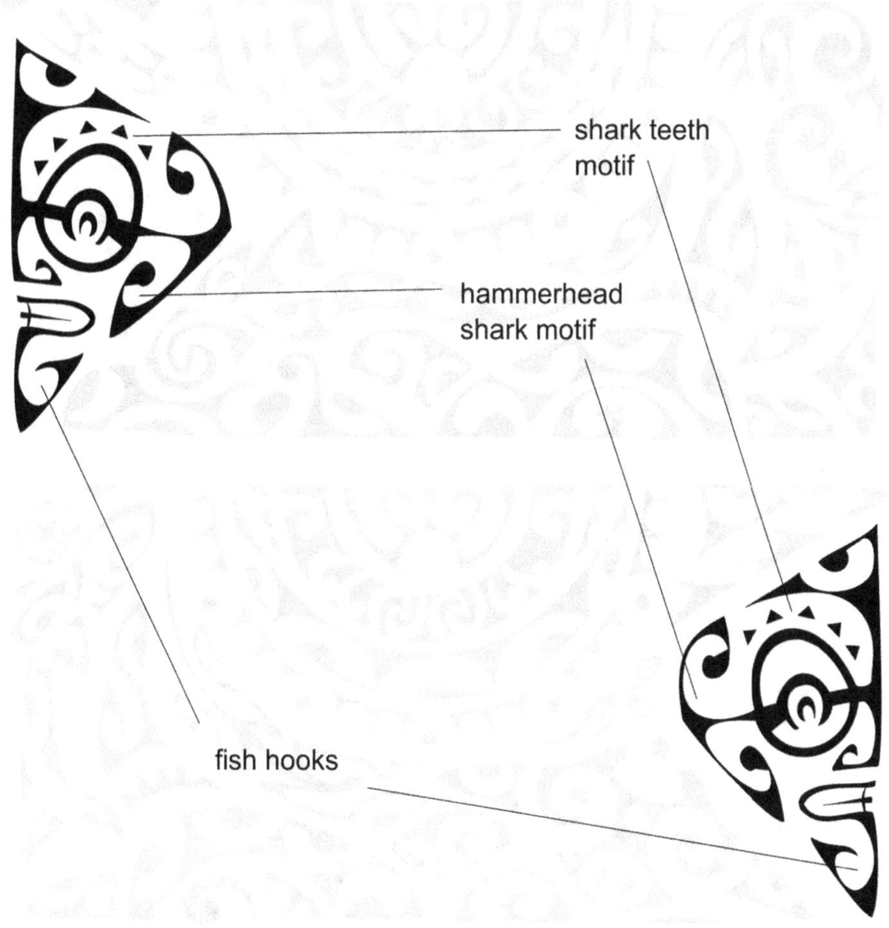

Other elements are specific to each armband to symbolize that even if they become a whole, they still have their individuality, brought into the family to make it complete.

Jakub's armband includes a hammerhead shark (determination, tenacity and strength), a manaia (protector, guardian angel) and two chasing pigeons (help granted to the dear ones):

Anna's one has a manta (beauty, elegance), a shark (adaptability), a Marquesan cross for harmony, a lizard and a small gecko (luck and health).

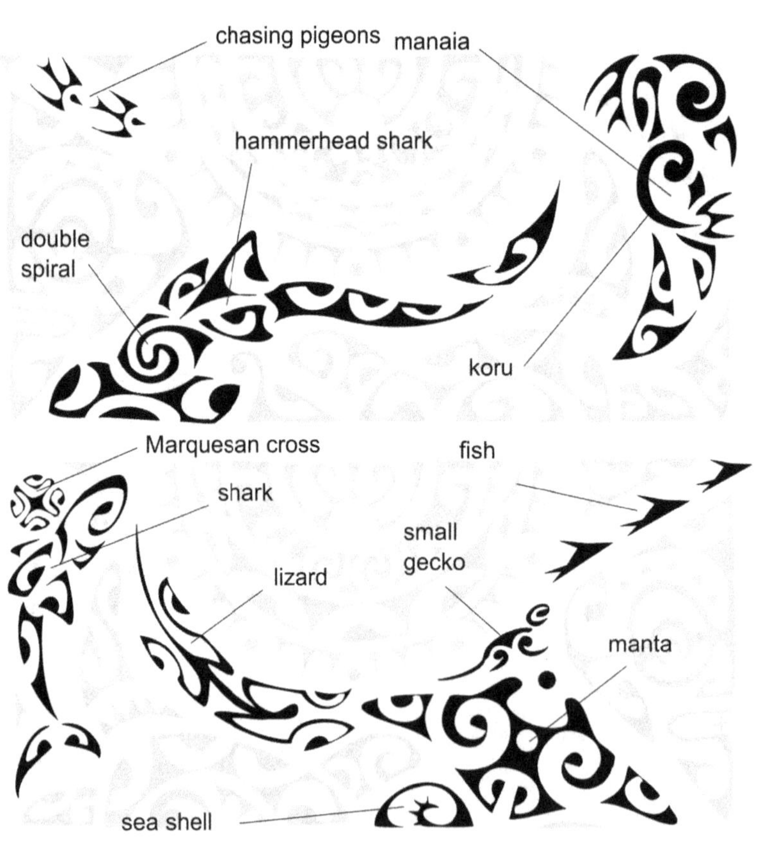

Domiziano's half sleeve

Domiziano requested a short sleeve tattoo for his left arm to represent some important things in his life.

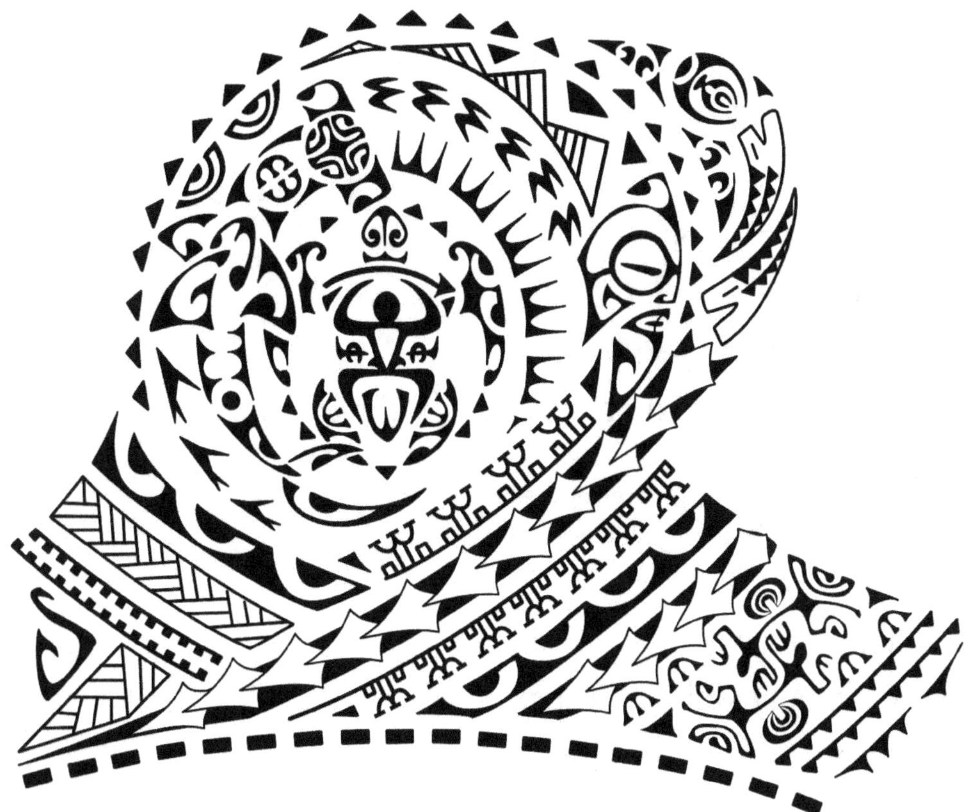

Requested meanings and elements:

Importance of family, tenacity, determination, travels, fights he has won (semi-pro fighter and self defense instructor), protection against adversities, good luck.

step 1: deciding the appropriate elements

Turtle: family

Spear heads, kena: warrior, fighter, strength

Warrior mask: defiance

Hammerhead shark: tenacity, determination

Enata: friends and foes

Waves: change

Sun: success, positivity

Birds: travels

Fish, fish hook: prosperity

Tiki, all-seeing eye, tiki hands and eyes: protection

Eels: adversities

Lizards: good luck

Ipu: fertility

Mountains: stability

Shark teeth: adaptability, protection

Braid: union

Standing stones: achievements

step 2: deciding how to dispose them

This design is all about a fighter, by trade and by nature, a warrior and this has to be prominent in the design, which should flow along the lines of the muscles in order to enhance their look.

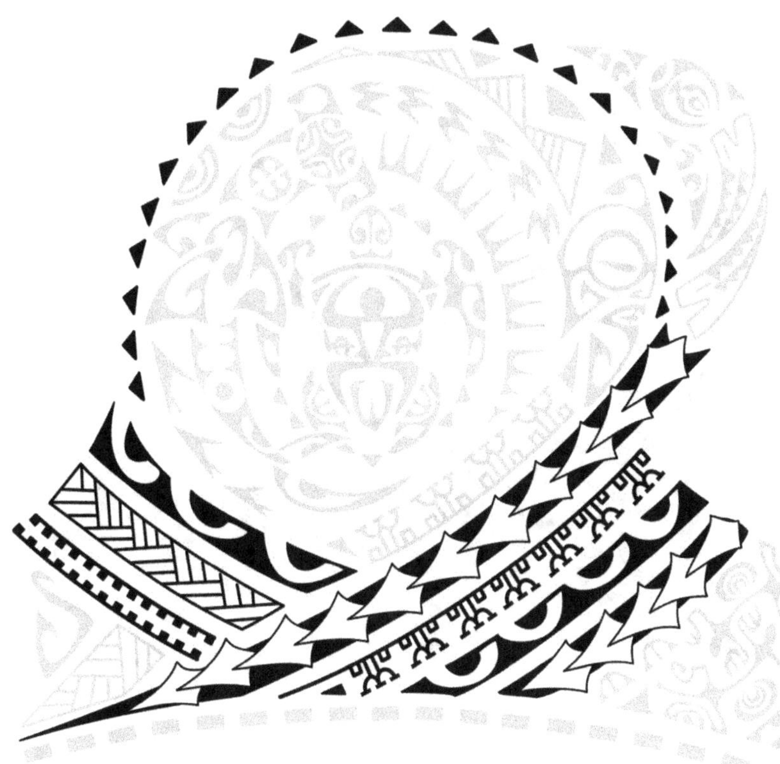

Main characteristics are strength, determination, valiance and tenacity, which have been symbolized using the hammerhead shark, *kena* (the warrior holding a spear over his head) and spear heads. The warrior itself is shaped to recall a warrior mask with his tongue stretched out as a sign of defiance to enemies.

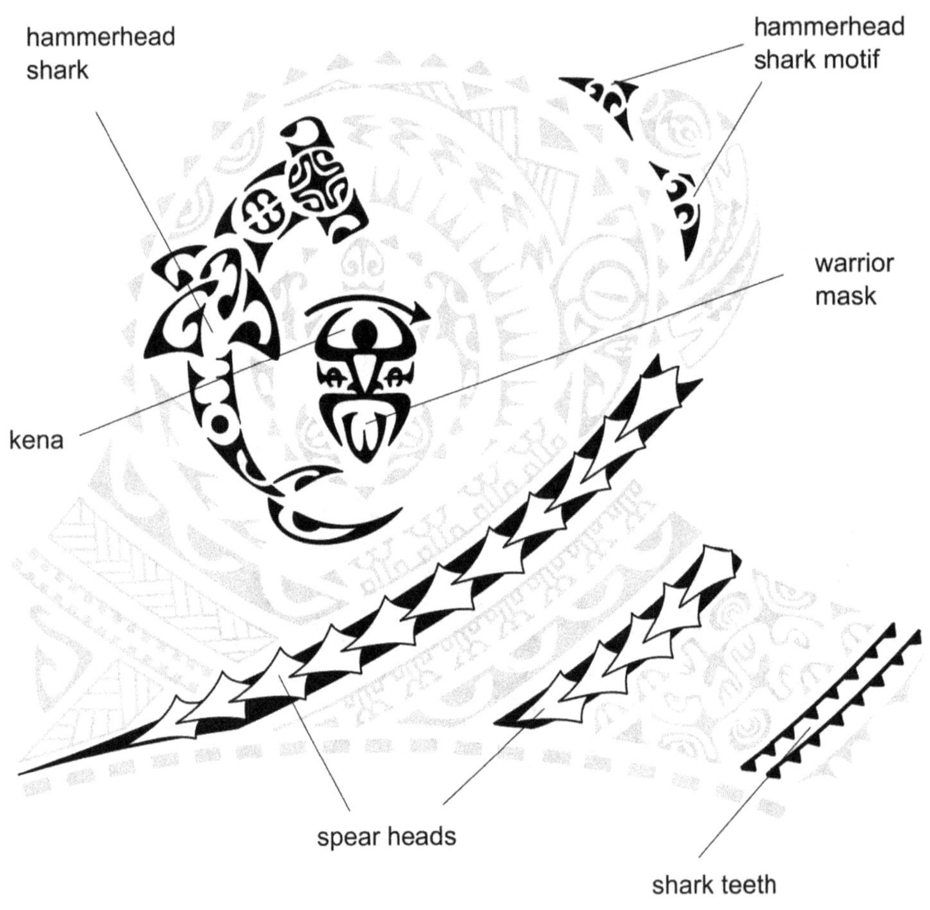

Protected in the middle of his life to symbolize its centrality, the turtle represents his family, with the double warrior being its shell guarding on it and protecting it from every change (waves shaping the front flippers).

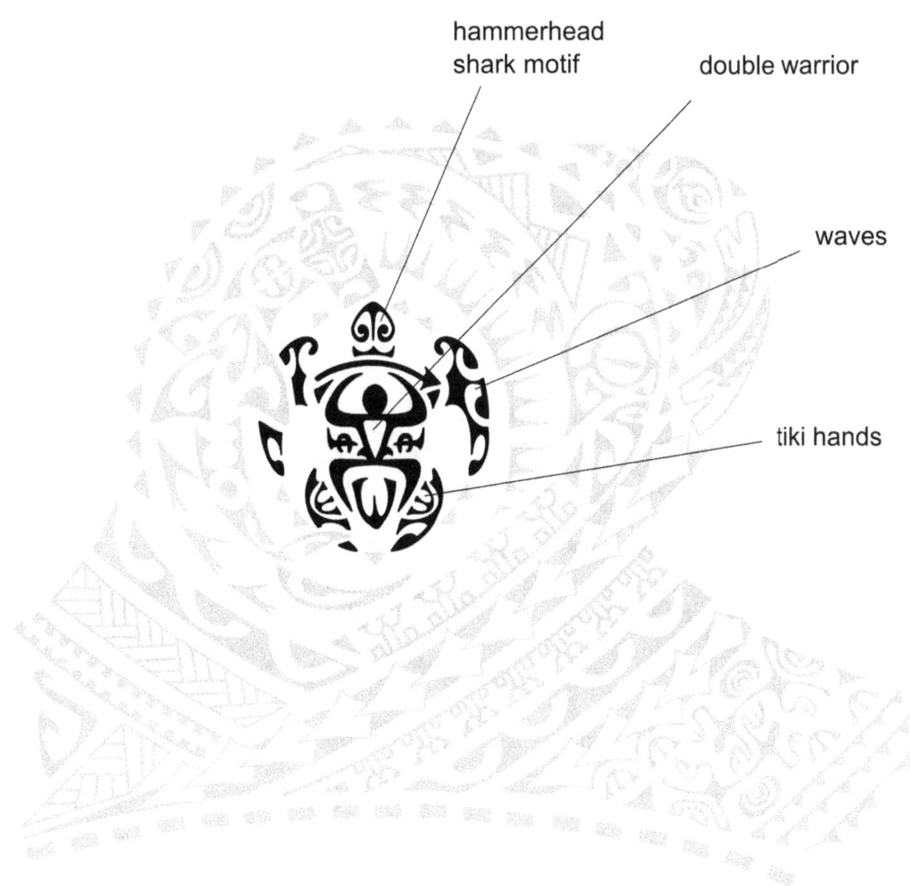

The turtle is also surrounded and protected by a hammerhead shark (determination, protection) on the left and by a sun (joy, positivity, success) on the right. Another sun made of shark teeth (adaptability) is on the outside, enhancing these characteristics.

There are several protection symbols in this design, such as *tiki* hands and eyes and the all-seeing eye on the back of the shoulder which, together with a *tiki*, keeps past difficulties (the moray eels) at bay.

One of the eels is pointing upwards and the other one downwards to symbolize the spiritual and physical challenges he faced and defeated in the past.

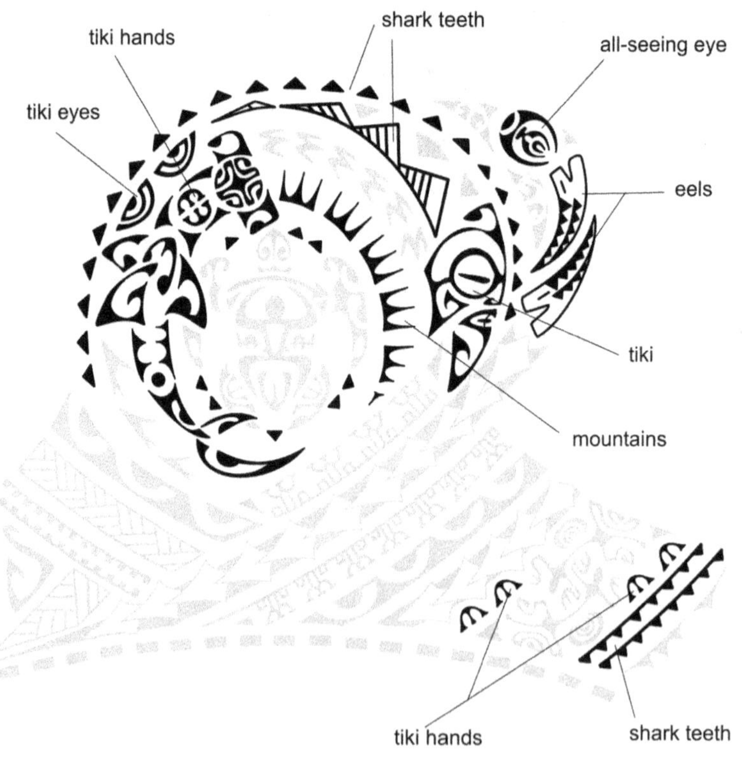

Birds and fish in this tattoo symbolize freedom, help and prosperity, all flowing around the family; a Marquesan cross was added for balance and harmony and lizards for good luck. The path of Kamehameha represents the hard path leading to prosperity (the fish hook) and the row of standing stones at the bottom of the tattoo represents the achievements on which Domiziano has built his new life.

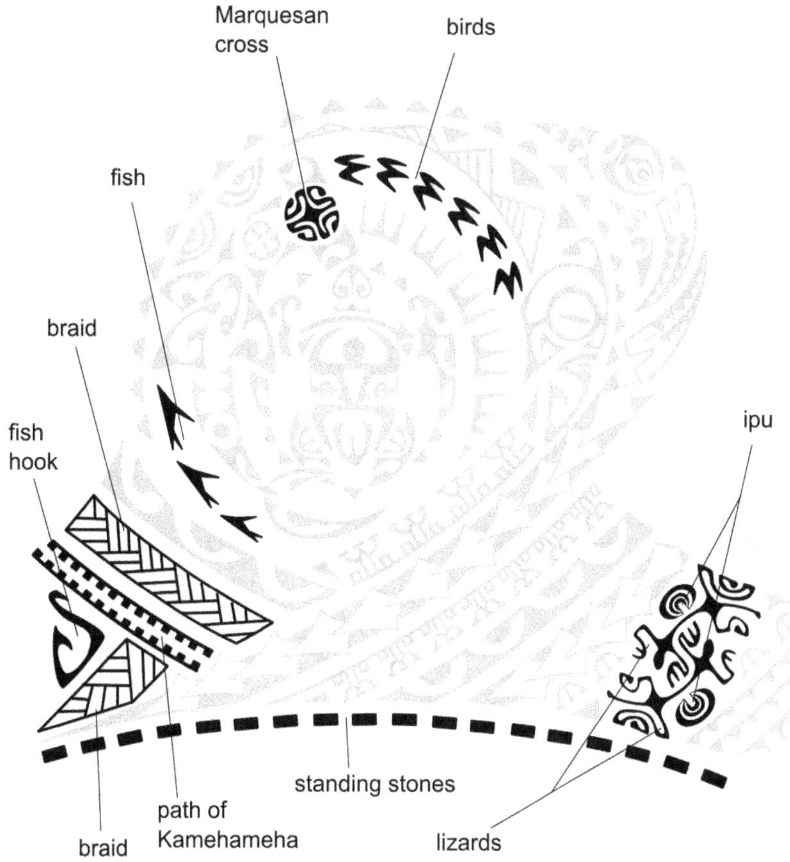

One row of spear heads in the armband has two similar rows of elements above and below, mirrored to each other. They are two rows of *enata* (men): the lower row of men, turned upside down, represents the adversaries defeated by Domiziano (together with difficulties and negative changes represented by the waves going down on the back of the arm), kept far and at bay. Above, the standing men represent true friends (fewer but bigger) who are closer to him, inside his inner circle, along with the waves going upwards symbolizing positive changes.

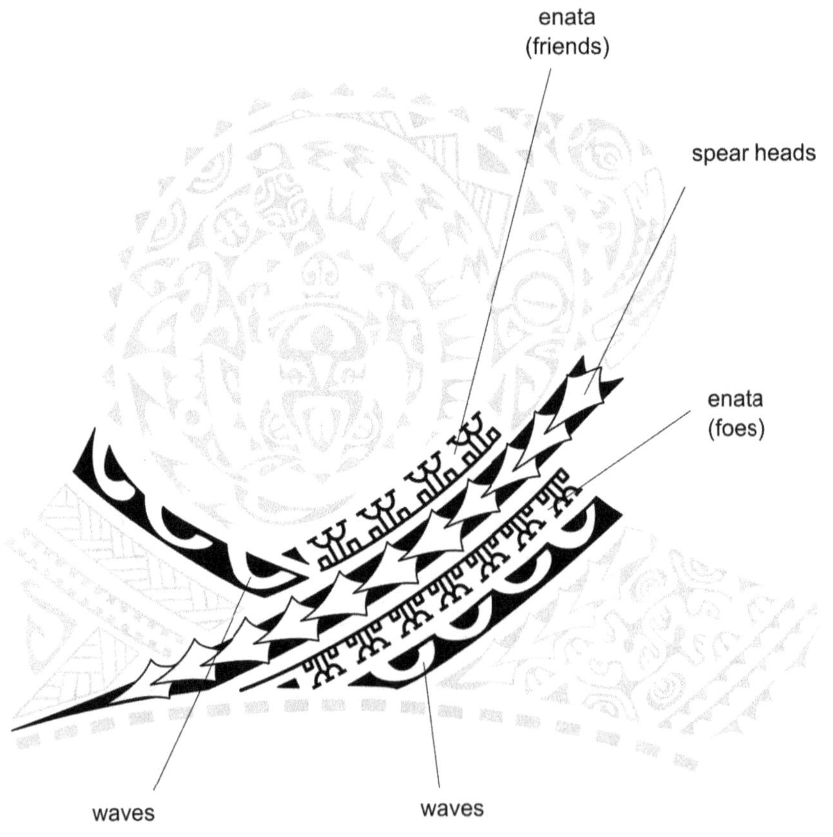

Poulomi's fire

Poulomi requested a design for her left arm, from shoulder to bicep, to represent her and some important people in her life.

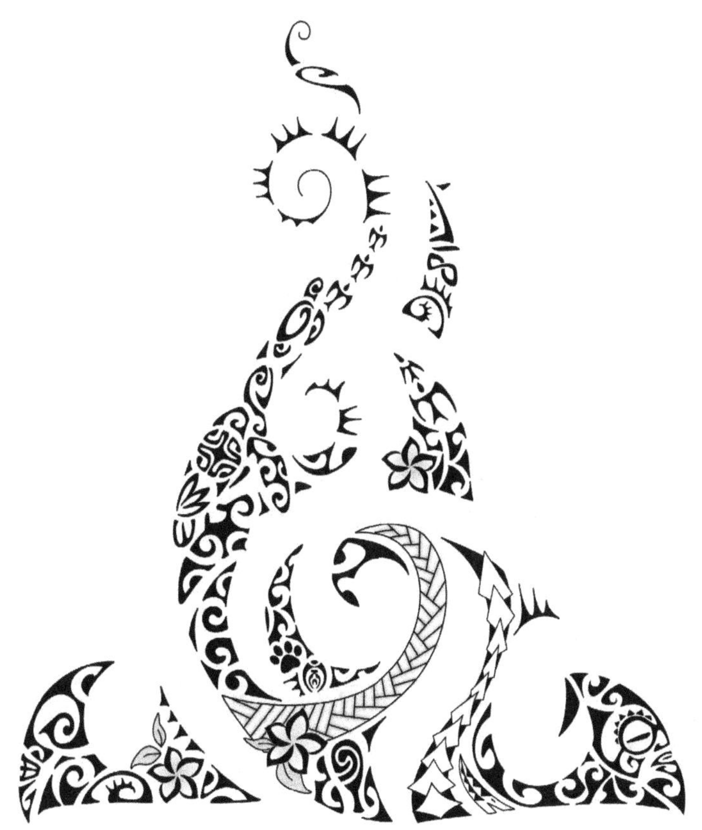

Requested meanings and elements:

Fire as the ruling element, change, courage, passion to fight for one's beliefs, her boyfriend and dog, her family members.

Her grandpa is dearly missed and was the protector of the family, her grandmother is a caring, loving person and her mother nurtured her and brought her up for the best. Her dog brightened many moments in her life and is now in need of her help on account of diabetes.

step 1: deciding the appropriate elements

Fire: passion, ruling element
Tiki: the protector
Frangipani flowers: the women of the family
Mere: respect
Braid: union
Turtles and flax leaves: family
Spear heads: strength, courage, the warrior
Waves: change
Chasing pigeons: help granted when needed
Hammerhead shark motif: determination, tenacity and strength
Manta: freedom, protection and elegance
Sun: positivity, energy
Koru: new life
Fish hook: prosperity
Sea shell: love and safe shelter, intimacy
Shark teeth: adaptability
Moray eel: difficulties

Mountains: stability

Twist: eternal love

All-seeing eye: protection from evil

+ 2 non Polynesian symbols:

Paw print: dog

Sailboat: sailing

step 2: deciding how to dispose them

Since fire is Poulomi's ruling element, reflecting much of her character and the passion she puts into her beliefs, we decided to shape her tattoo like a flame going up the arm. Similarly to her life, which is made of the moments lived with her dear ones, the flame was made by the union of smaller flames representing them.

The three frangipani flowers symbolize femininity and represent the three women of the family; a touch of colour may be added to them to represent the beauty of life.

The main flame represents Poulomi and from bottom to top (from matter to spirit) we find: hammerhead shark motif (determination and tenacity, strength), manta (freedom, protection and elegance), turtles (family; a Marquesan cross inside the first one is for harmony, the flax leaves are for union and a *tiki* hand is for protection). The birds represent freedom, watching the world from a higher perspective and they lead to the sun (positivity, joy and success), shaped like a *koru* to represent a new beginning. The top elements are a fish hook (prosperity) and another stylized *koru*.

At the base, close to the right flame representing her grandfather, a mere (a short club held by chiefs) represents the respect she has for him.

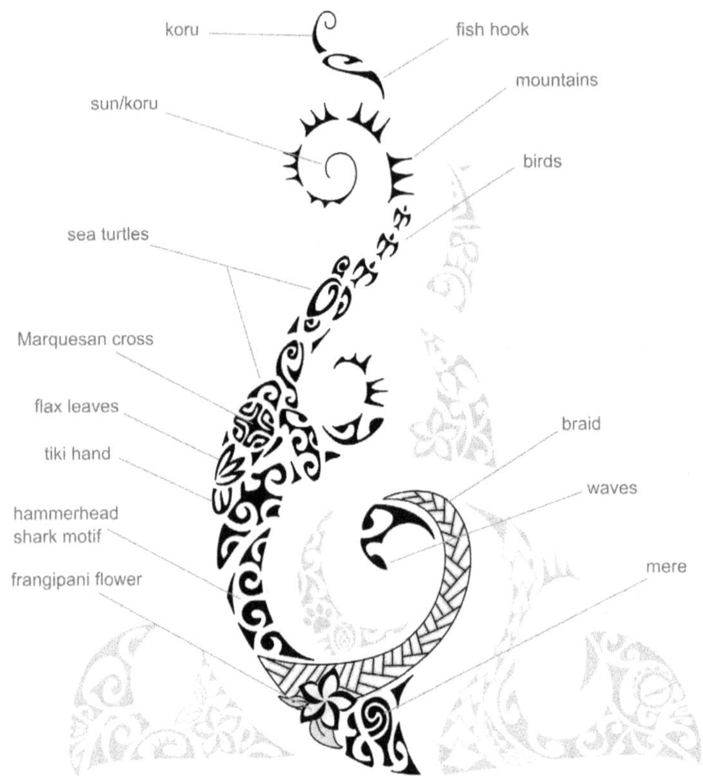

Next page, the big flame on the right shaped like a fish hook (prosperity, status) represents her grandfather Sati Nath (a maorigram of the letters SN appears inside of it). He was the protector of the family (the *tiki* facing outwards).

The moray eel pointing down represents the material difficulties he has fought and overcome with strength and courage (the row of spear heads and the hammerhead shark motif representing determination and tenacity, traits that make him and Poulomi similar).

His path starts close to Poulomi's one; they apparently got divided (symbolized by a wider space between their two flames) but in the end got closer again. Where their paths meet again, Poulomi's flame is shaped like a koru (new beginning) and made of waves (change) and braid (union, to symbolize he'll always be with her).

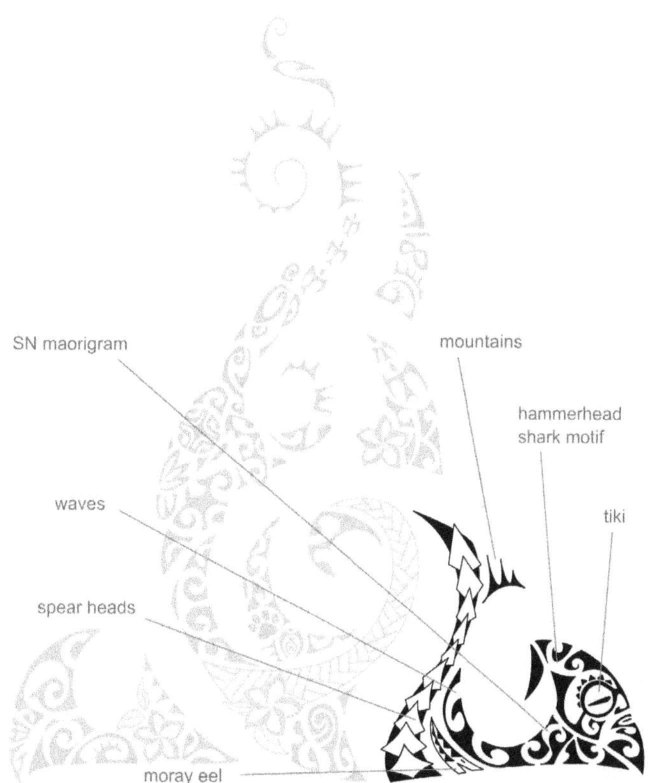

The flame on the left represents her grandmother Purabi (we placed a P maorigram in it, on the left of the sea shell). The sea shell represents love and safe shelter, intimacy and the shark teeth represent adaptability and strength. The *tiki* guards Poulomi and, together with the one representing her grandfather on the right, protects her from all sides in the past and in the future.

Her grandparents' flames are positioned at the base of the design to embrace her and be her foundation.

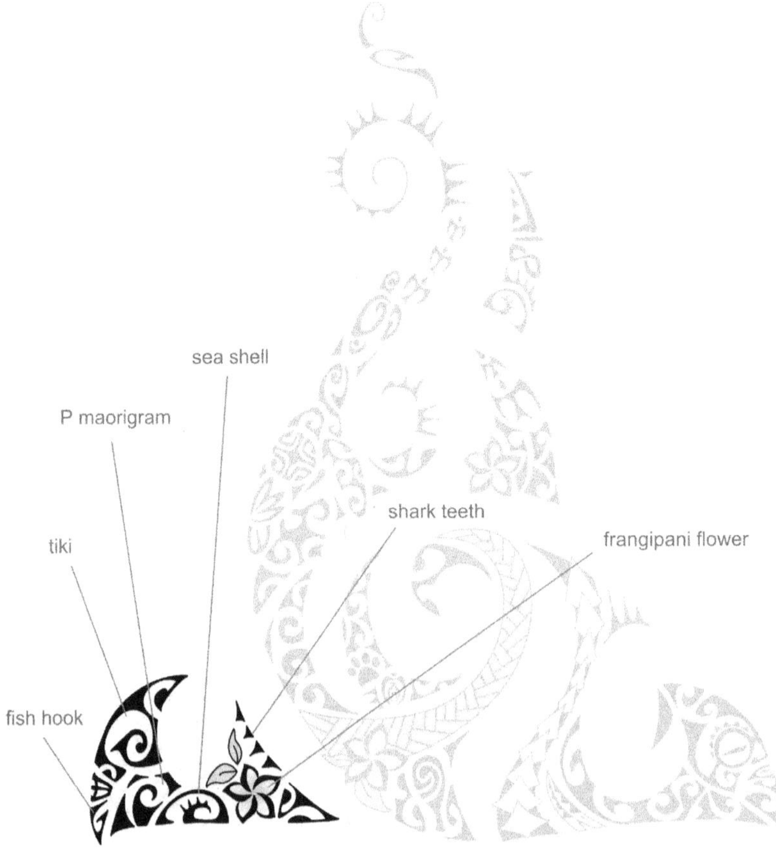

Kasturi is Poulomi's mother (K maorigram next to the flower): the two birds following each other represent how she'll always be there to help Poulomi whenever help is needed. Close to the left, on Poulomi's flame, mountains symbolize she represents stability for her.

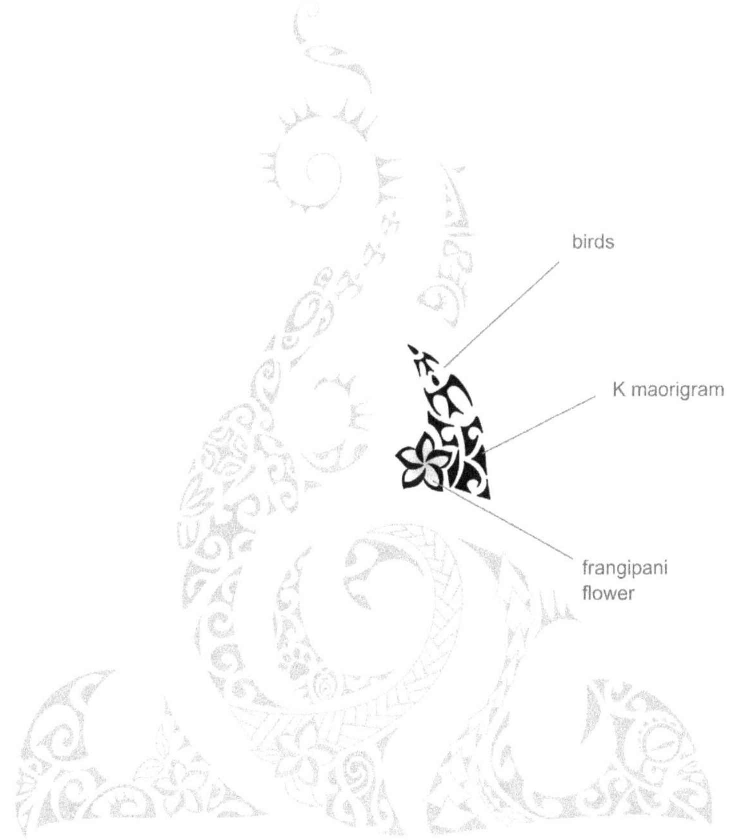

Going up we find the flame for her boyfriend: the sea shell is for love and intimacy, mountains for stability and a twist for eternal love and union. A stylized sailboat completes the flame together with shark teeth (protection on the sea).

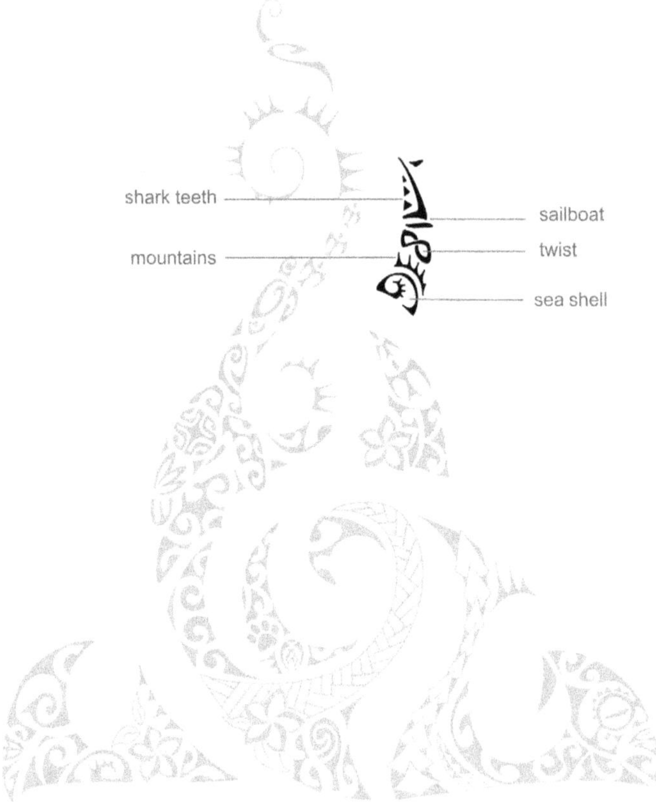

The stylized sailboat and the paw print are not Polynesian designs but they represent a nice example of how non-traditional elements can be actually incorporated in a more traditional design without compromising the general look and feel of the tattoo.

The first 4 flames surround Poulomi's one because they represent people who protect her; one last small flame was placed on the inside of her one because it represents her dog Khushi, who gets protected by Poulomi instead.

It has a K, the paw print and the all-seeing-eye to ward evil off. Mountains are to wish him stability among changes (the waves).

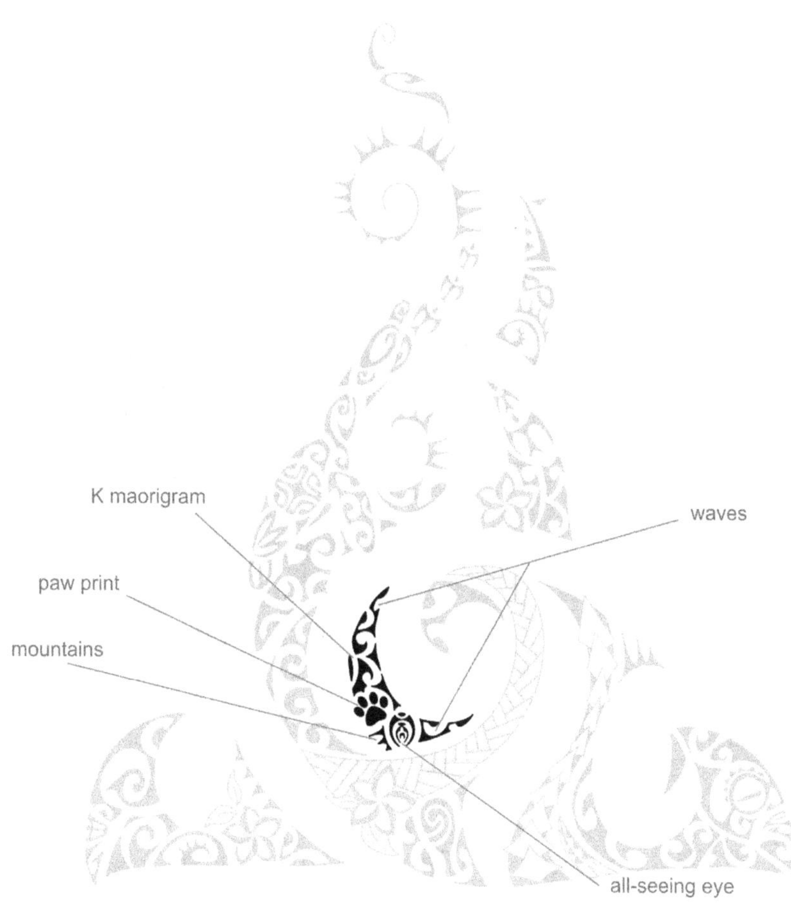

Michelle's ankle tattoo

Michelle requested a design going around her ankle down onto her foot, with three plumeria flowers (one for loved ones lost and two for her children), symbolizing new beginning, love of the sea, love, strength, happiness and balance in life.

Requested meanings and elements:

Three plumeria flowers, new beginning, love of the sea, love, strength, happiness and balance in life, to go around the ankle.

step 1: deciding the appropriate elements

Ipu: ancestors
Sun: happiness
Shark teeth: strength
Sea shell: love
Koru: new beginning
Seagull: higher perspective
Waves: the sea
Marquesan cross: balance
Turtle shell motif: family
Plumeria flowers

Step 2: positioning them

The biggest flower of plumeria was placed on the back of the ankle because it is related to the past and it represents ancestors (same meaning has the *ipu* symbol on it, as well as descent and fertility).
The sun around the ankle bone (eternity and joy) is made of shark teeth (strength, adaptability) with a turtle shell motif representing family and joining here the plumeria of Michelle's ancestors to the two smaller ones of her sons.
The sea shell is for love, intimacy and safe shelter, the *koru* is for new life and waves were added to symbolize the love of Michelle for

the sea.

The seagull on top represents freedom and watching the world from a higher point of view.

The Marquesan cross joining the two smaller plumerias of Michelle's sons represents balance, union of the elements and harmony, which is what they represent for her.

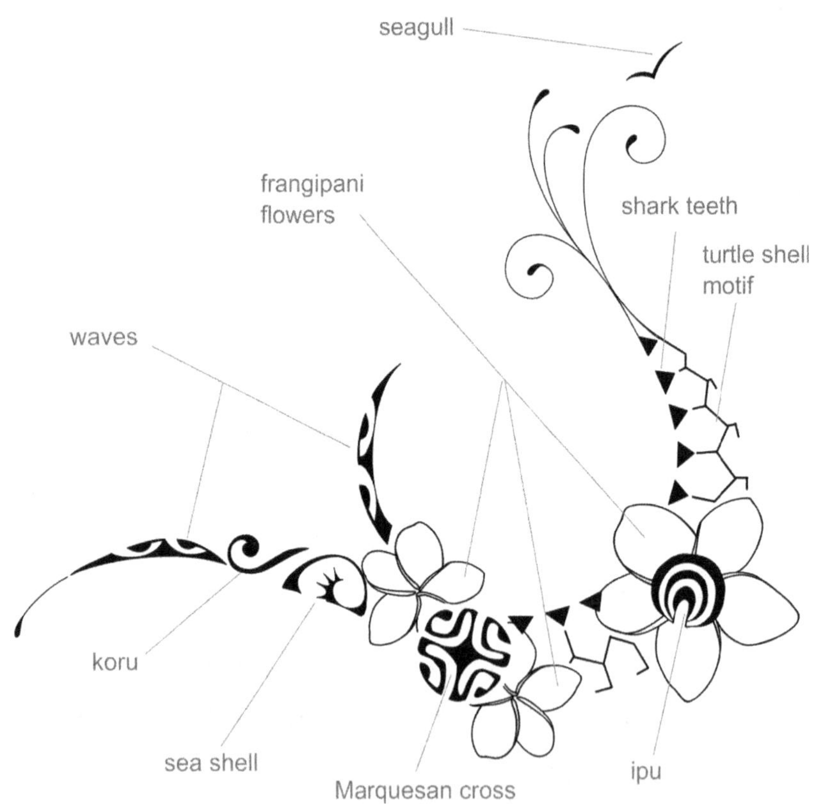

In this case we used a few non-traditional elements again to refine the design (the swirls on top); inspiration was taken from hibiscus flowers and the round shape of the swirls makes them similar to *koru* elements, with the upgrowing sprouts representing new life and growth.

Titiro, whakarongo, korero

"Look, listen, then speak"

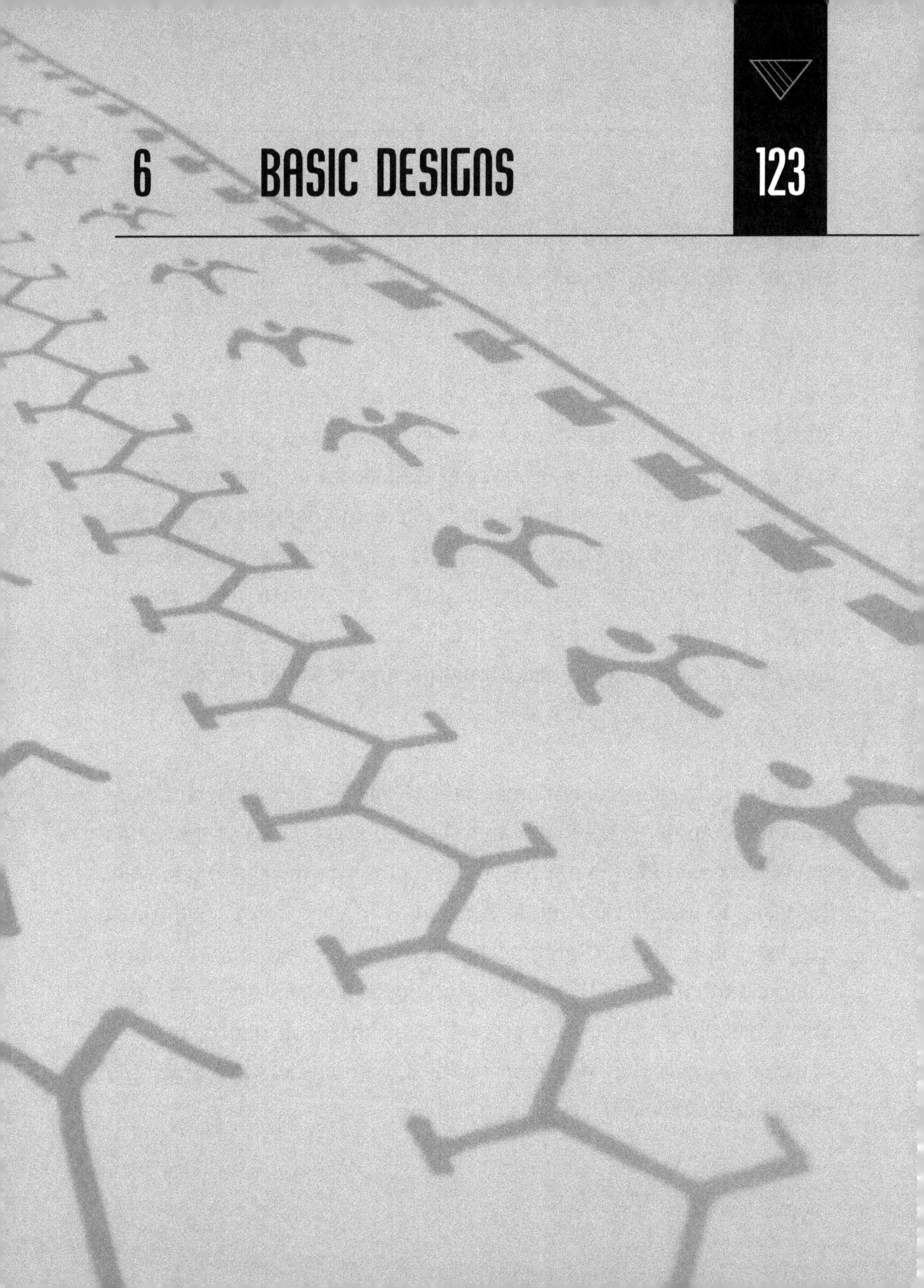

"Titiro, whakarongo, korero"
—Look, listen, then speak

The following designs are very simple and they can be used as "building blocks" to create as many new designs as creativity allows to. The empty outlines can be used at the start of the creation process (see previous chapter) to help decide elements positioning and they can later be filled with dedicated motifs. If you are using the designs from this chapter, we do suggest you to customize them anyway instead of using them as they are because a personal touch will always be the best way to make a unique and personal tattoo.

These are a few shapes, but creating new ones is very easy with basic skills of computer graphics: search the web for a photo of the animal you want to include in your design. The closer to the shape you want, the easier to work on it later. If you had to adjust a colour photo we'd suggest you a standard graphic program, but if you are working to prepare a tribal design then the best choice is a vector graphics one. The great thing about vector graphics is that you can change the shapes by simply dragging their outlines, without deleting, erasing or redrawing them and resizing is a snap too.

Shapes outlines and fillings are easily turned off and on separately so that you can just grab your animal, trace it (some programs have a very useful "vectorialize bitmap" feature that will help at this stage) and turn off the filling. Your outlined image is now ready to be embedded as a guide in your new design!

Birds

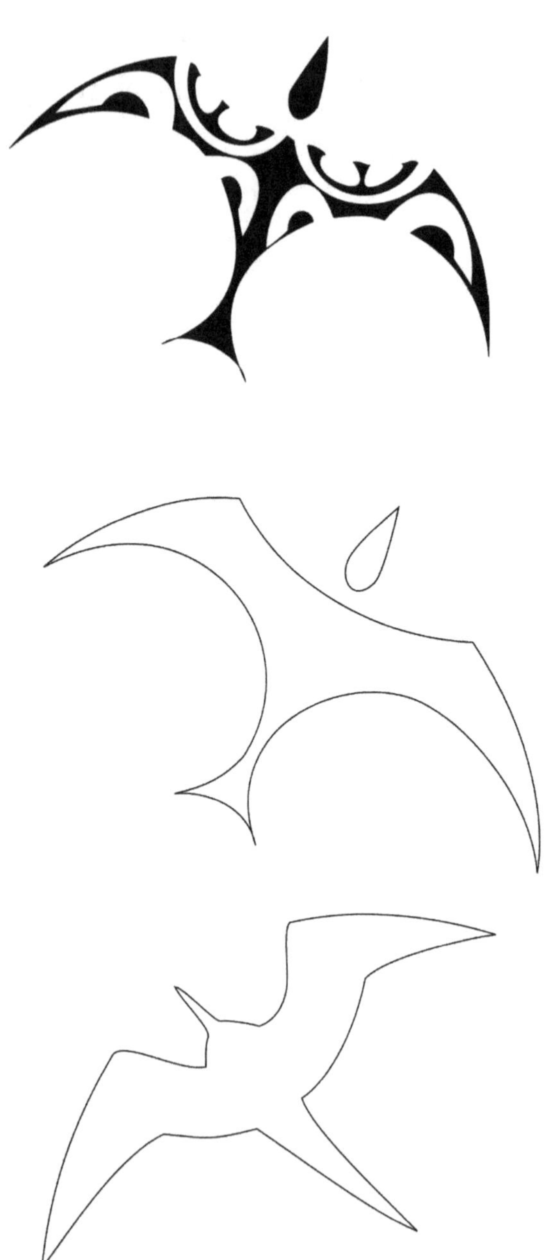

Mantas

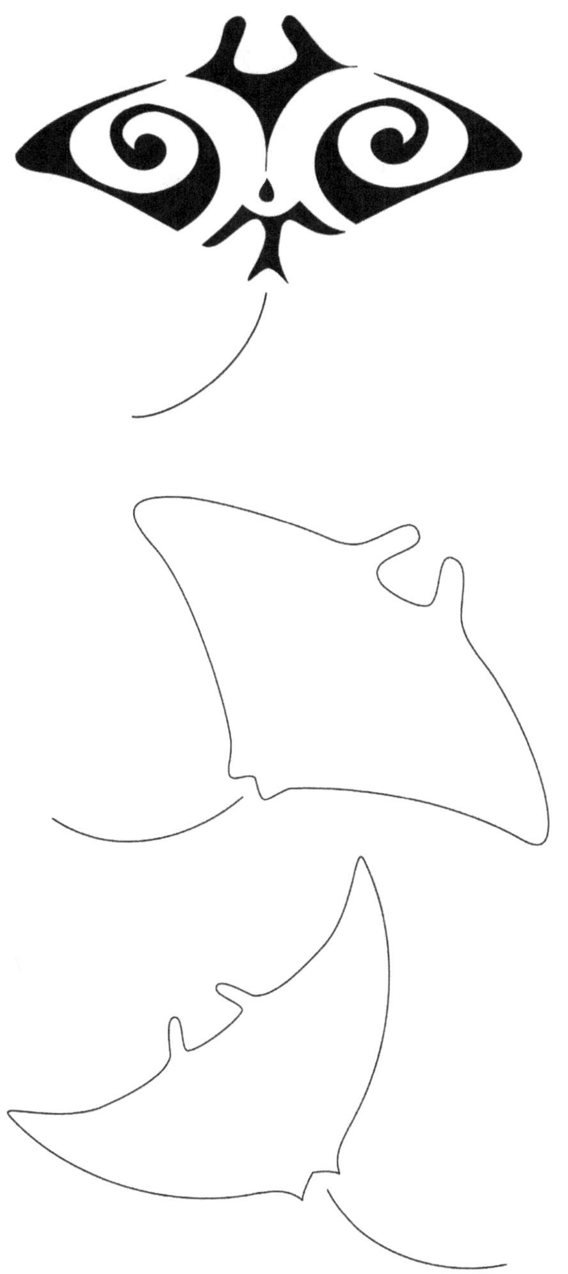

Hammerhead shark

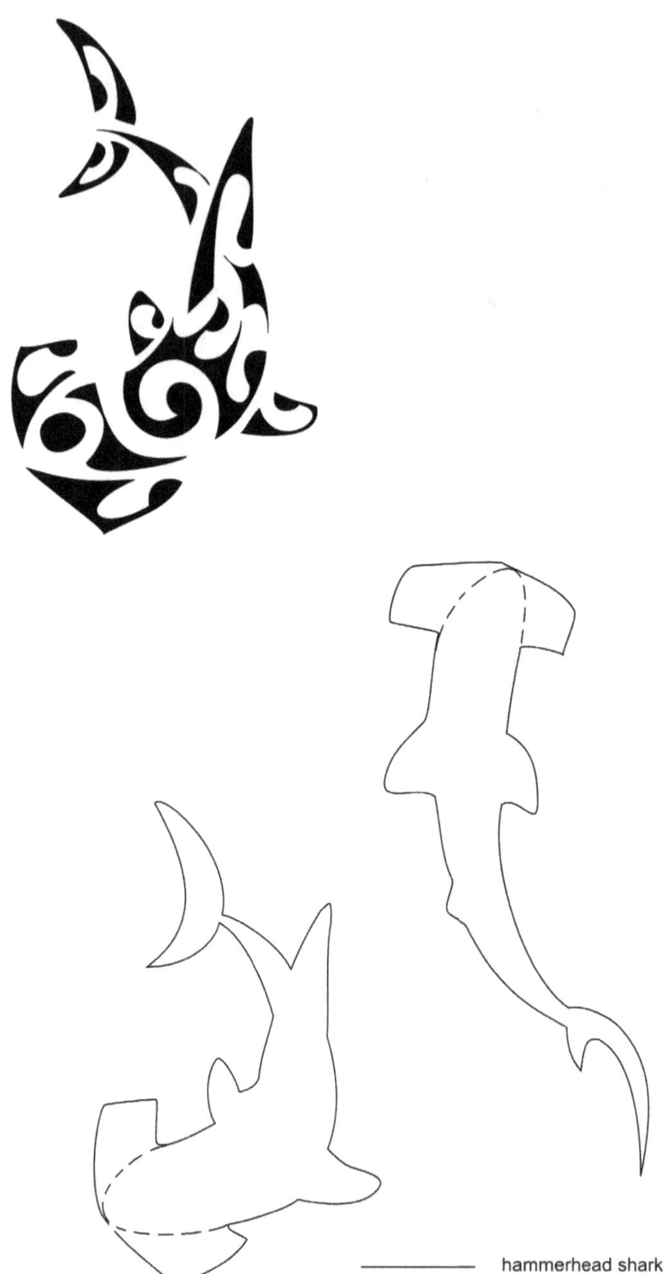

Dolphins

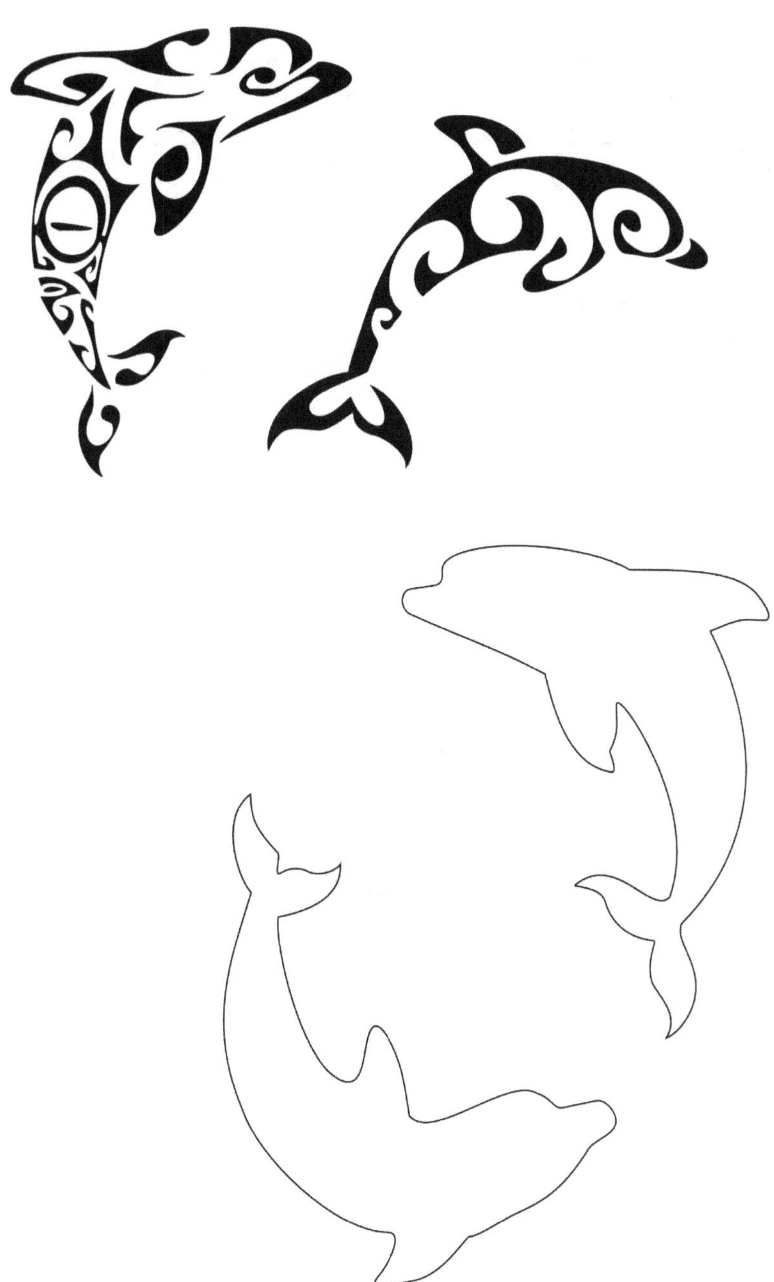

Turtles

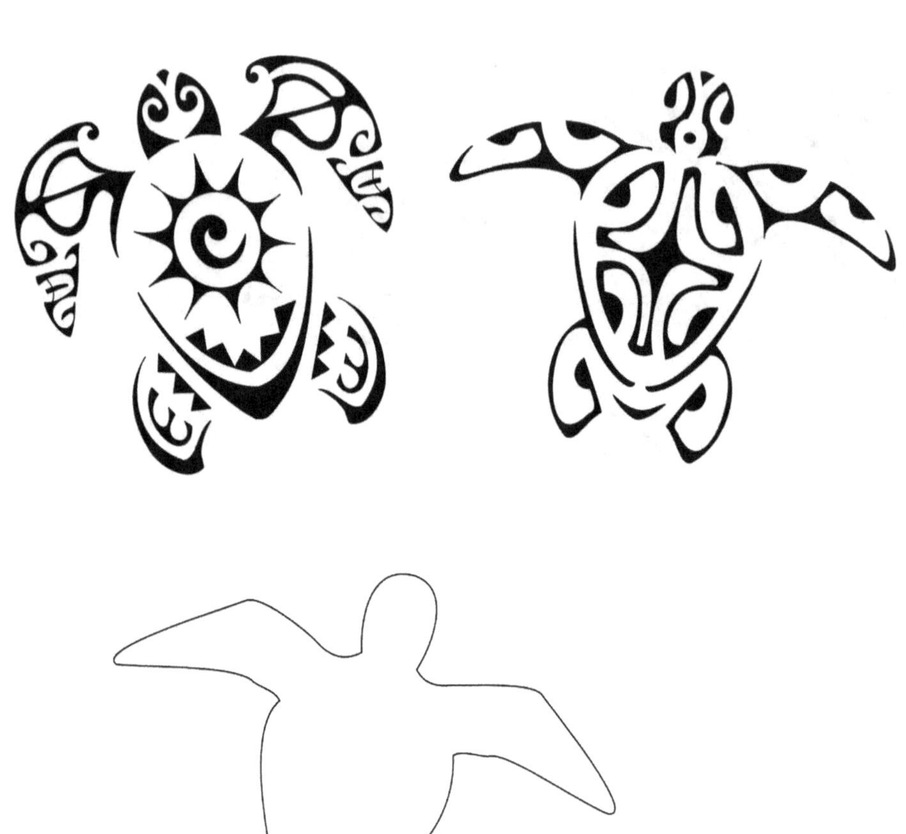

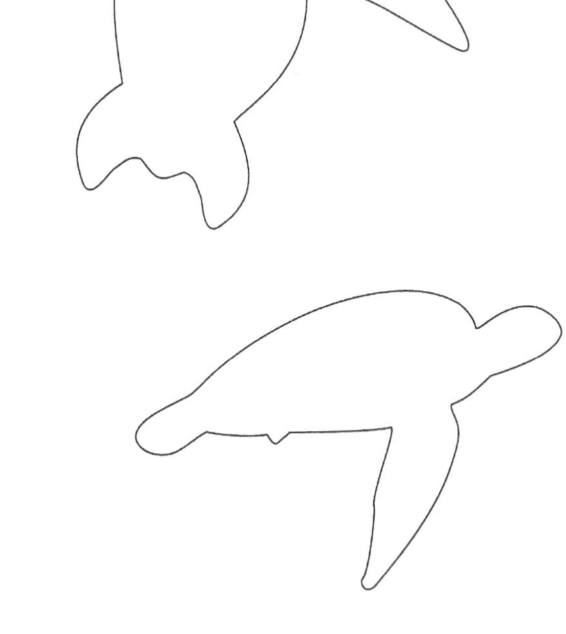

Seahorse

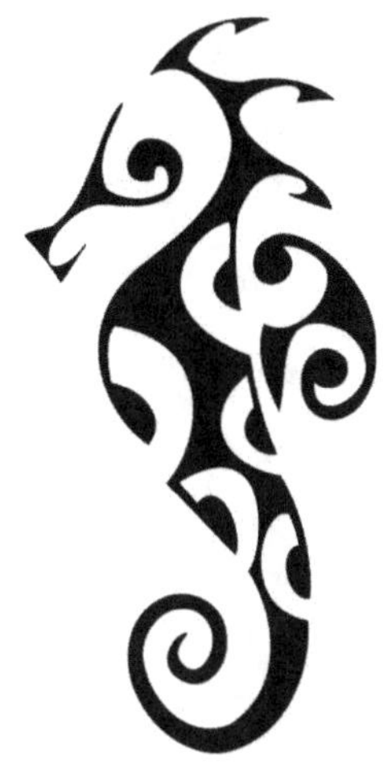

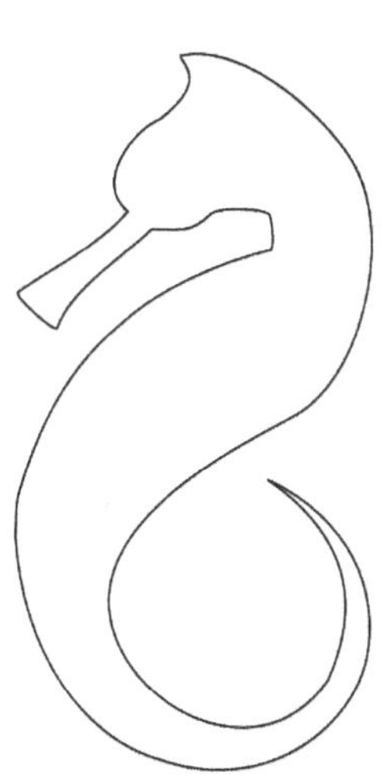

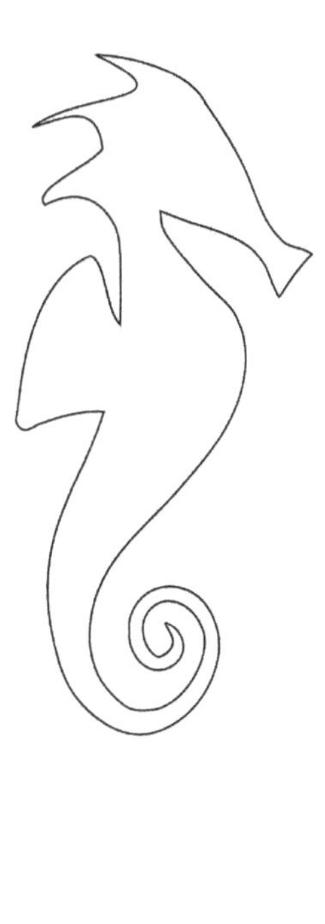

Gecko / lizard

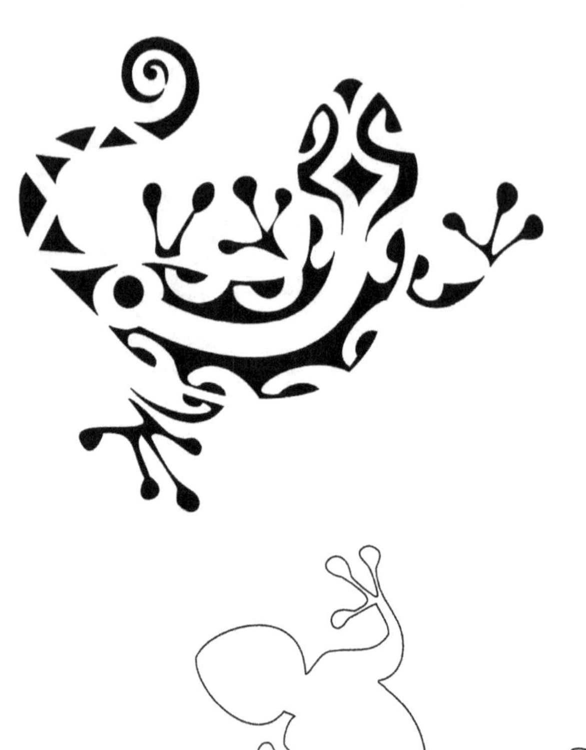

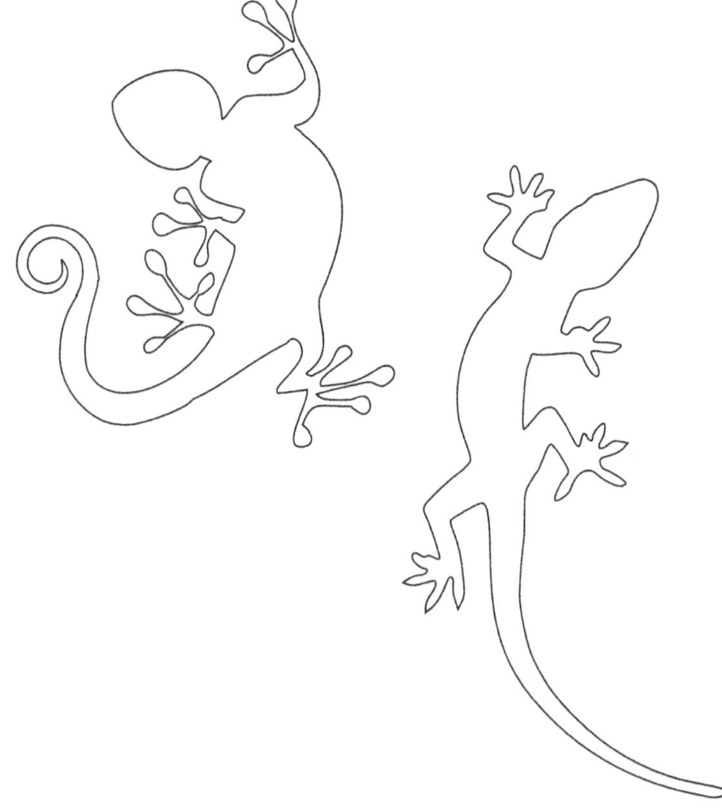

Frog

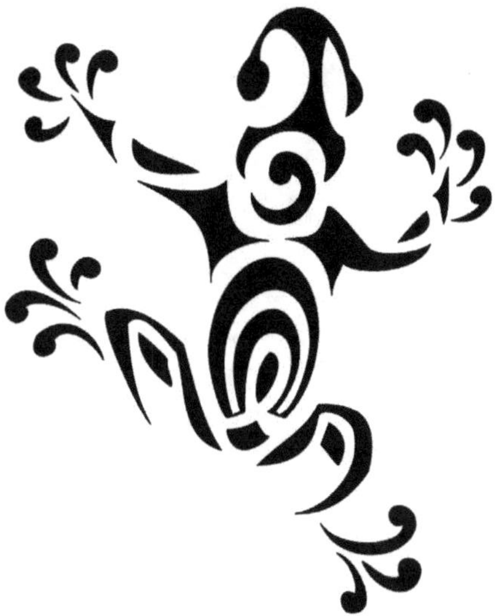

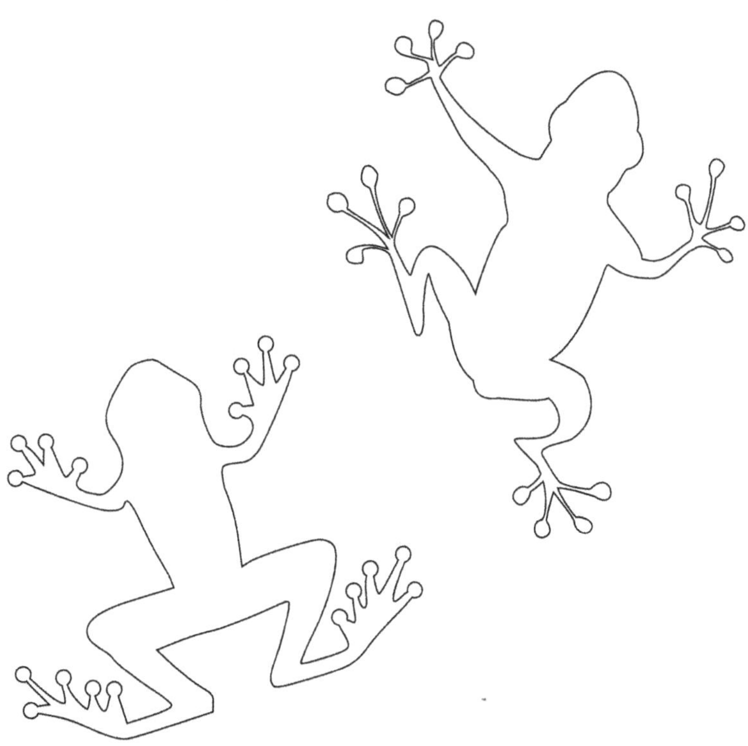

Sailfish / Swordfish

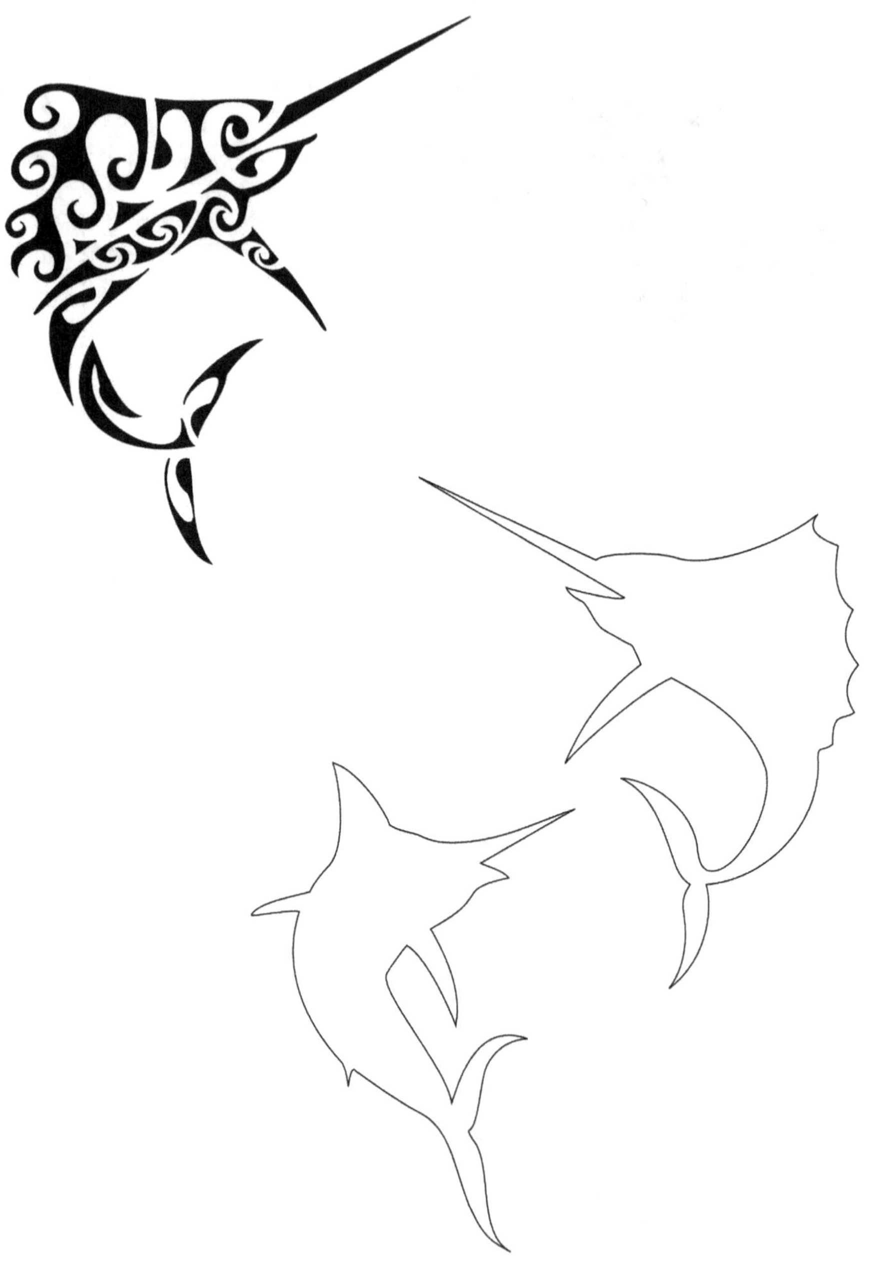

Jellyfish

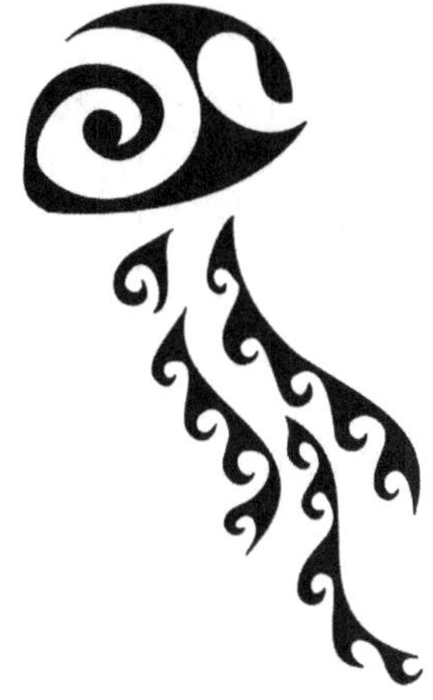

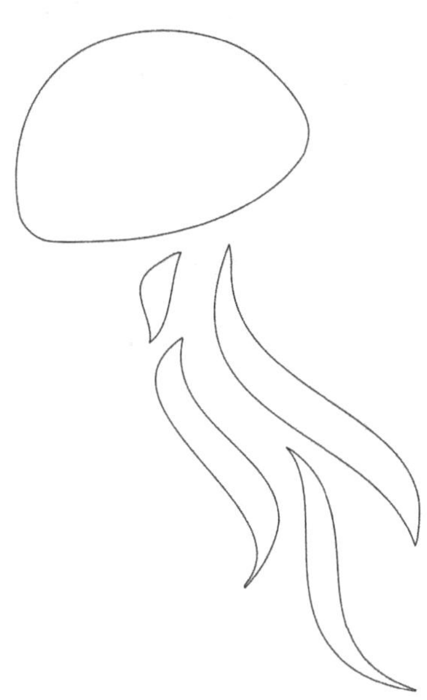

The first thing to know when writing a name in Polynesian style is that Polynesian people didn't have written alphabets.
There are no letters used by Polynesian languages so another way must be found to integrate letters from existing alphabets into a Polynesian design.

Basic elements

At Tattoo Tribes we decided to create the letters by composing them from basic elements that actually belong to Polynesian cultures, specifically chosen for their shape and meaning: the *koru* and the eye of the *tiki*; they are both extensively explained in chapter 3.

There are no fixed shapes and there are no standard designs that can't be varied and modified to your liking; this allows you to create ANY shape and ANY alphabet, just by means of this pair of symbols, more easily when using their stylized version.
Koru are particularly fit for creating blank shapes out of other elements and they actually serve this purpose in many Maori designs.
On this account, we call this type of writing "Maorigrams".

Koru:

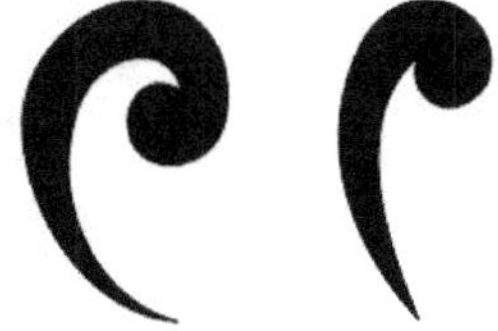

Tiki eye:

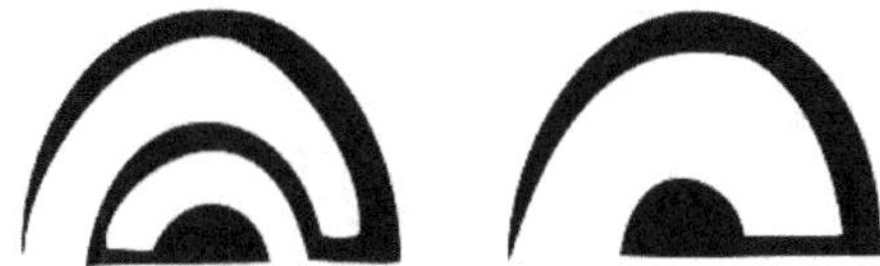

The best integration is obtained by leaving the letters as empty spaces inside a design that can be both solid colour or filled with traditional motifs. The latter solution gives the best aesthetical results as it can be seen in the following latin alphabet where a sample for the plain letter is on the left and the corresponding "cut-out" version with traditional-like fillings is on the right.

Latin alphabet

A:

 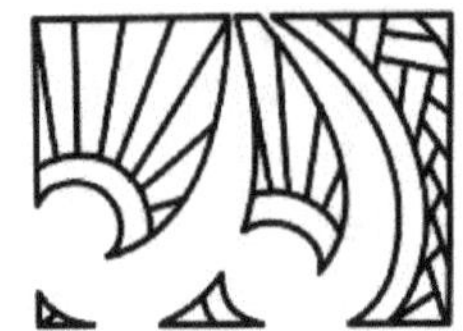

variant

B:

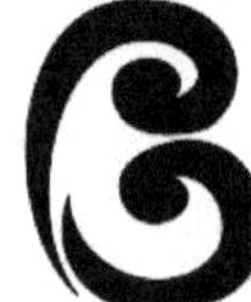 

C:

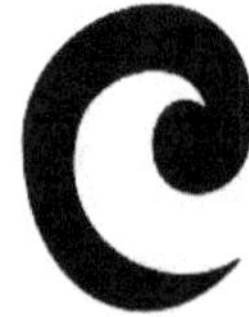 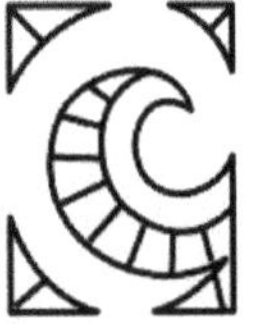

D:

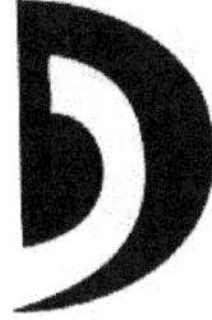 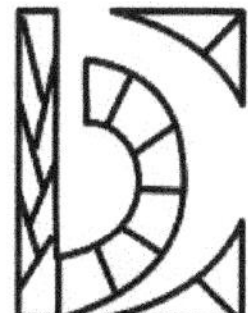

E:

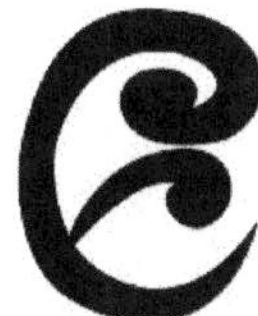 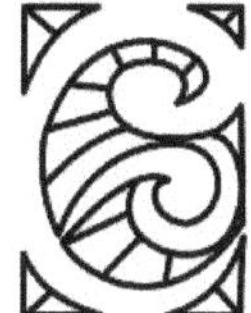

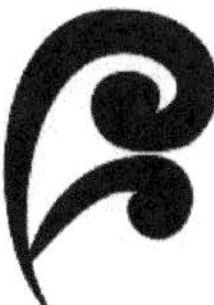

variant

F:

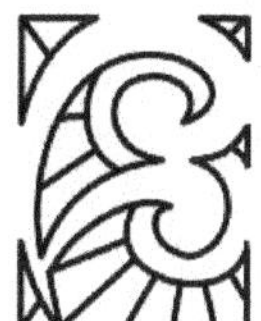 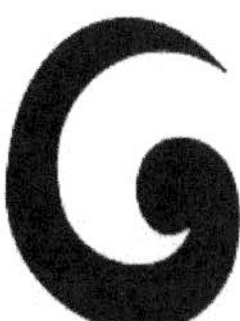

G:

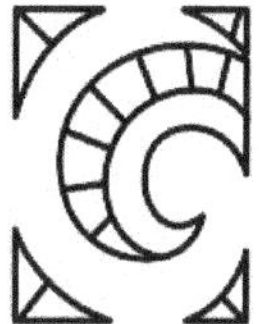

H:

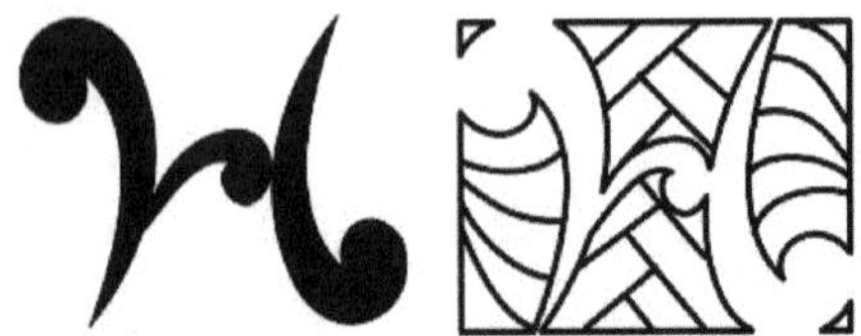

I:

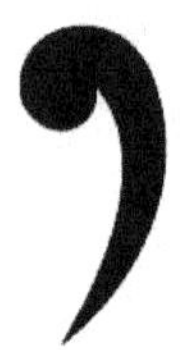 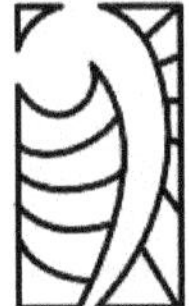

J:

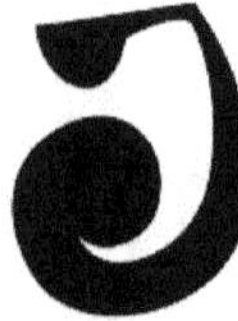 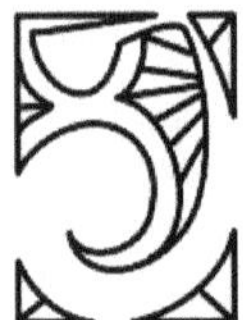

K:

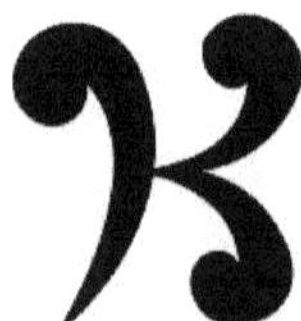 

L:

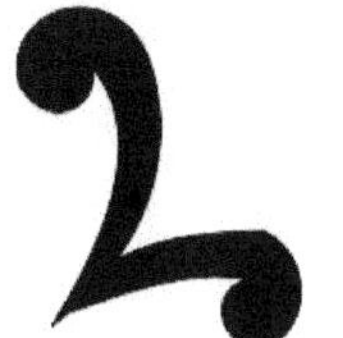 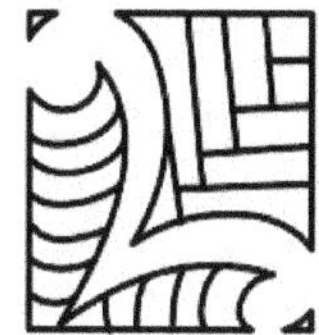

M:

 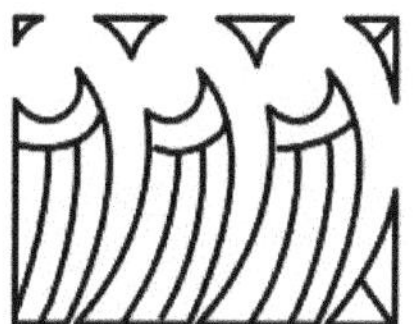

variant

N:

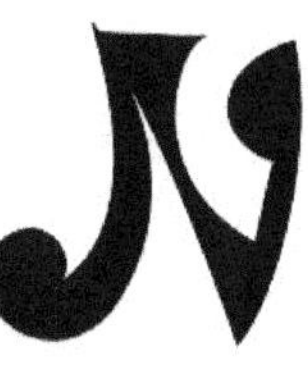 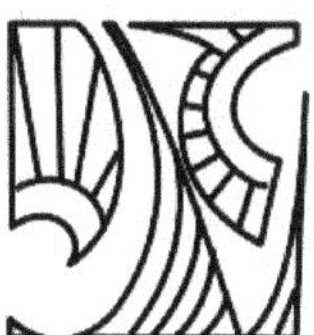

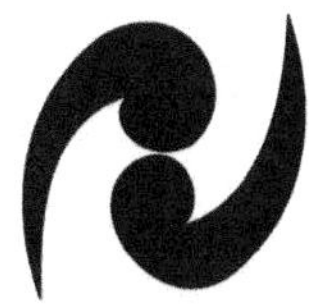

variant

O:

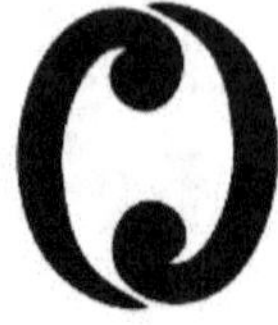 

P:

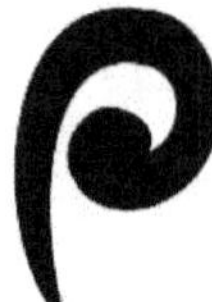 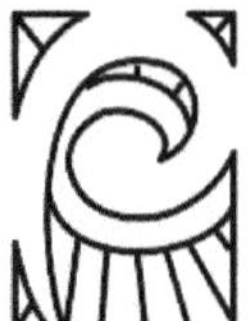

Q:

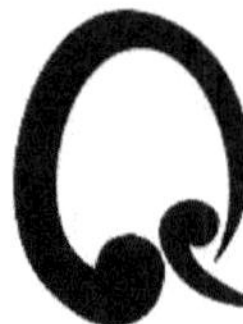 

R:

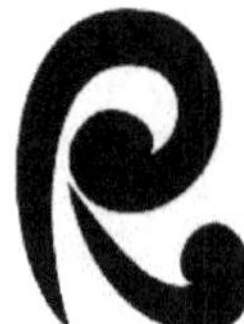 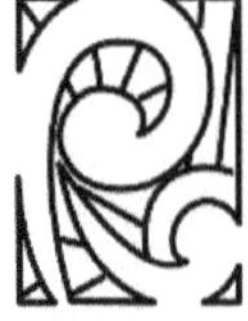

S:

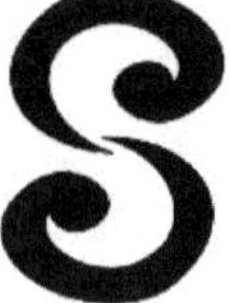 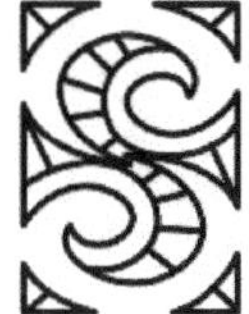

T:

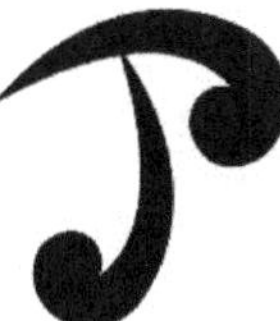 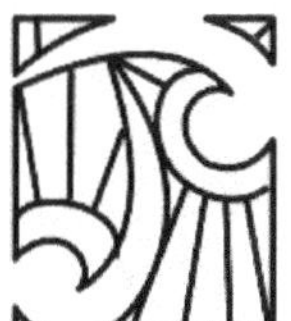

U:

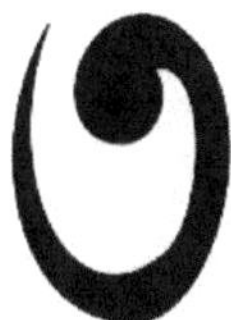 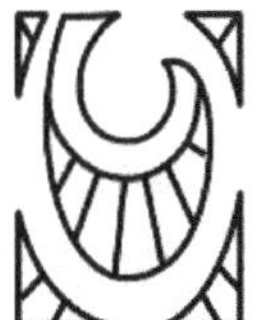

V:

 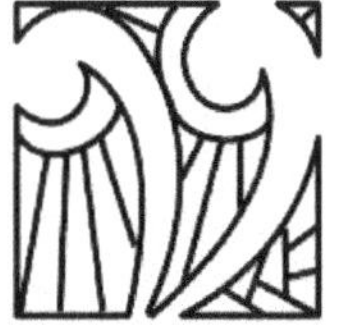

W:

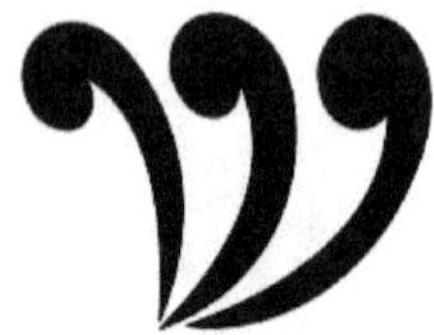 

X:

 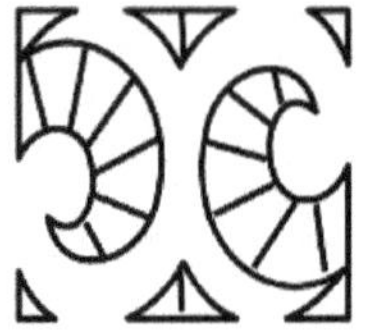

Y:

 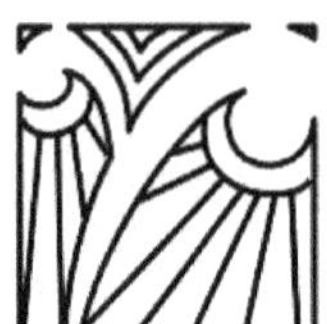

Z:

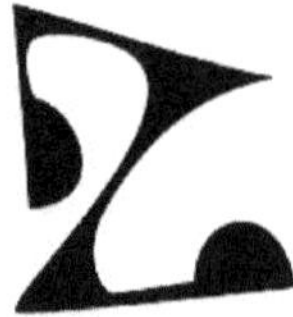 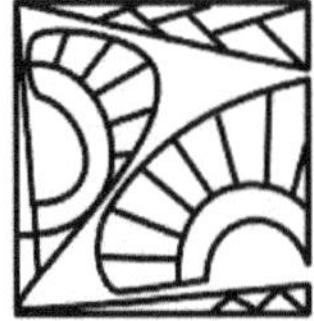

The creation process

When preparing a maorigram it's important to decide how clearly visible we want the letters to remain: a solid black filling will make the letters stand out, leaving them very easily readable, whereas a traditional filling will make them more integrated and partly disguised into the design.

The following series of different renderings of the same name "Bianca" shows incremental levels of disguise:

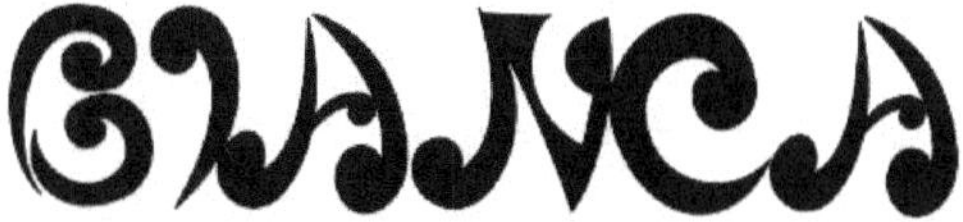

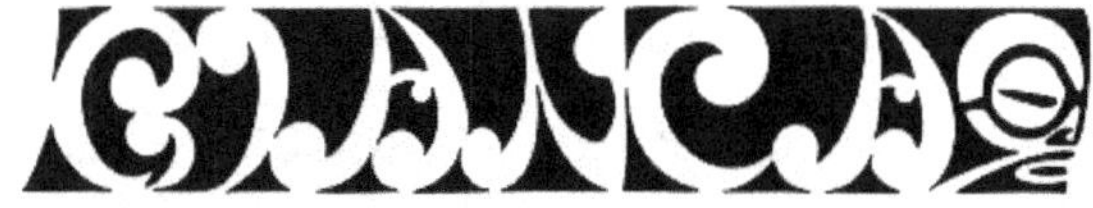

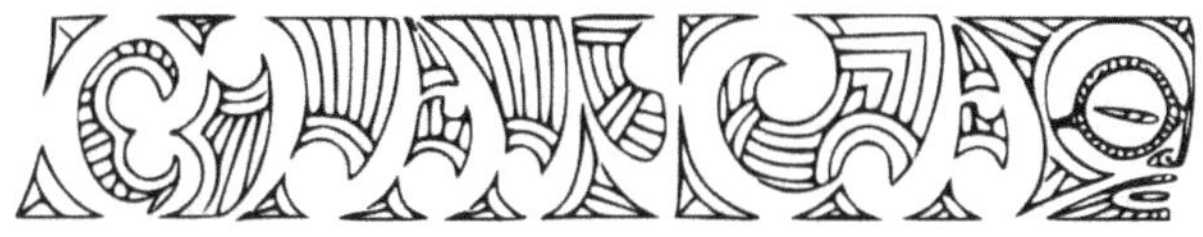

As shown, more elements can be added and integrated into the design to add meanings to it. In the example above the *tiki* was added to protect Bianca.

Let's see how to proceed creating a maorigram step by step.

1. Create a path where the Maorigram will go, usually two parallel lines (but of course any shape can be used). Border lines will help you make all the letters the same size. This path will give the final shape to your Maorigram:

straight path

rounded path

2. Start composing the word with the letters you created. We'll recreate the name Bianca using the previously given letters. During this step, just use the simple version on the left for each letter.

Place the letters close to each other, leaving a little more space to separate words if you have more than one; giving a light colour to both the path lines and the letters will help keep the final elements clearly identifiable:

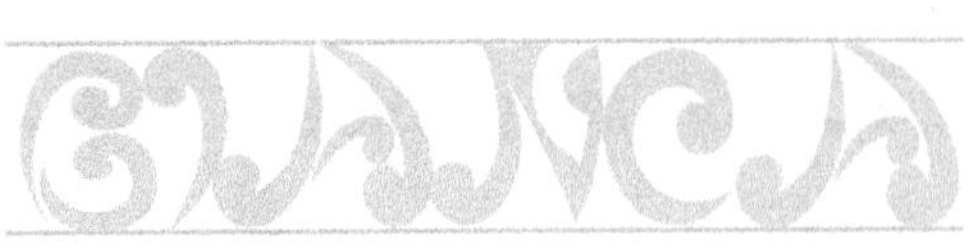

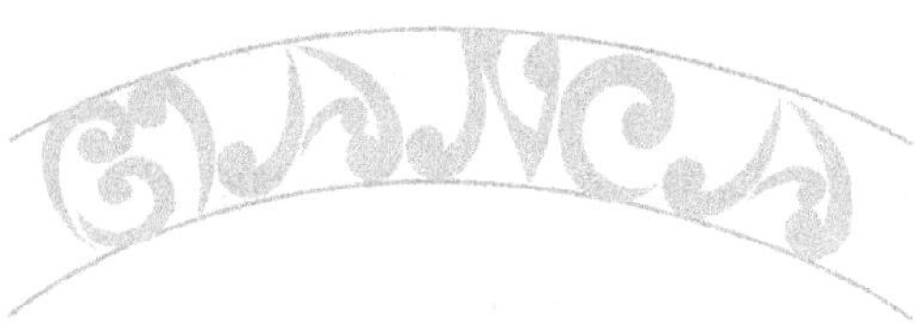

3. Outline with a darker colour all the elements included between the letters and the path lines:

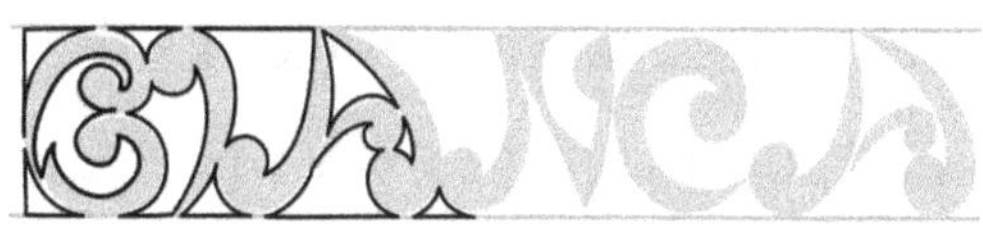

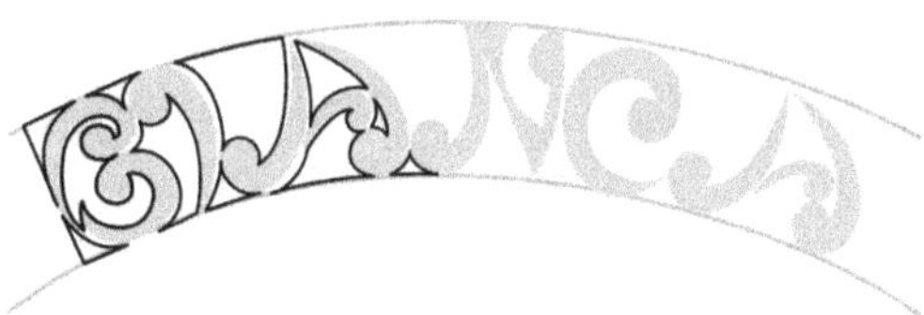

4. Remove path lines and letters keeping only the dark elements and decide the type of filling you prefer. The final result will look like this:

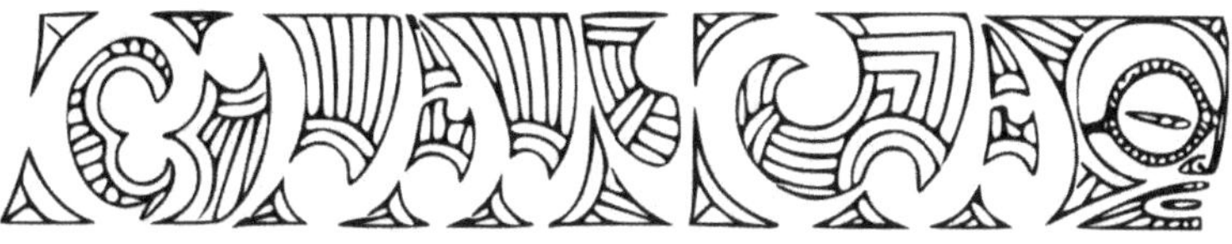

NOTE: the letters we prepared can be used "as they are" in their simple, solid version as a guide to create your own Maorigrams. The decorated versions are just to show how they may look, to give ideas, but they would not work well to prepare a traditionally decorated maorigram if they were simply placed next to each other: to create an organic design that does not look cluttered, the blocks between the cut-out letters must not have evident discontinuities, presenting a homogeneous filling instead.

Here is an example of what the name "Bianca" would look like if the decorated letters were simply placed side by side. Compare it with the final sample just below and you'll realize how much the filling can assist in making a beautiful design.

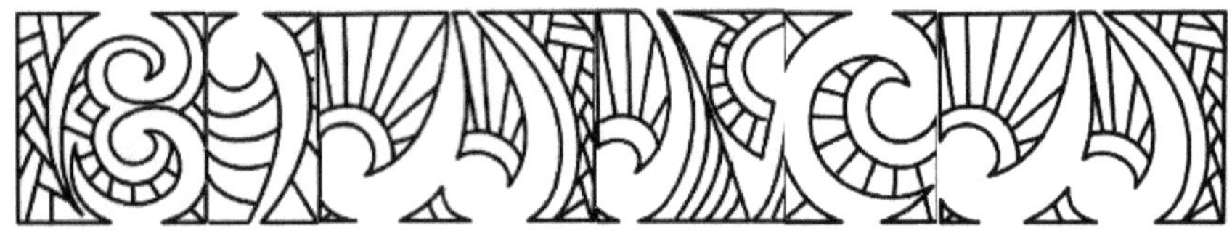

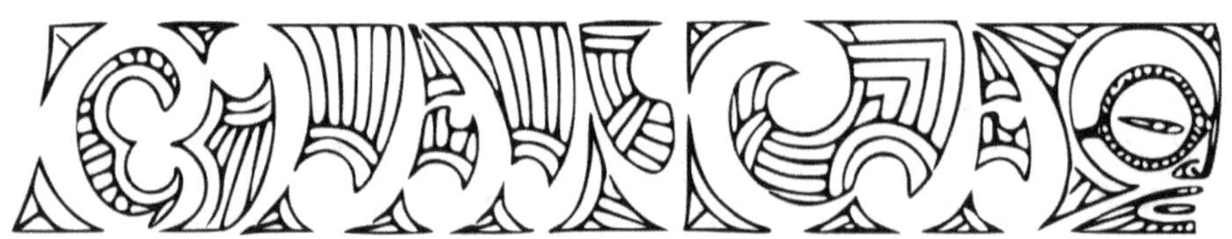

Samples

[1]   **MPG armband**

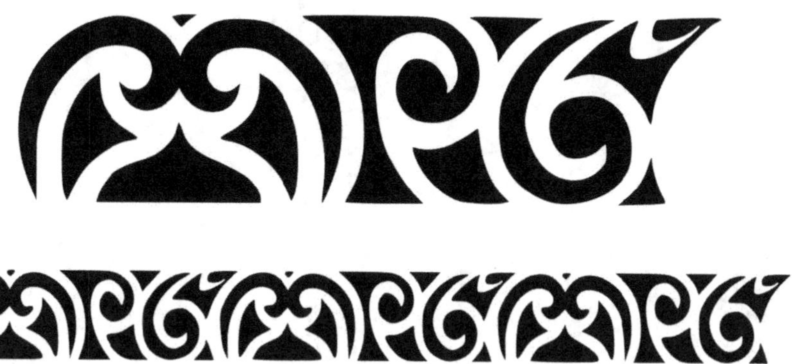

[2]   **Dragonfly**

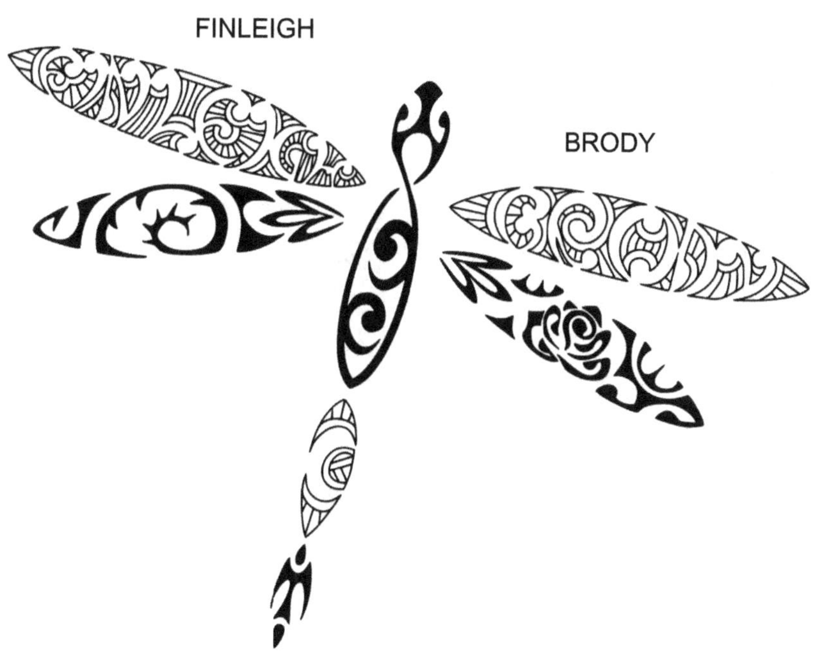

[3] **Latin sentences**

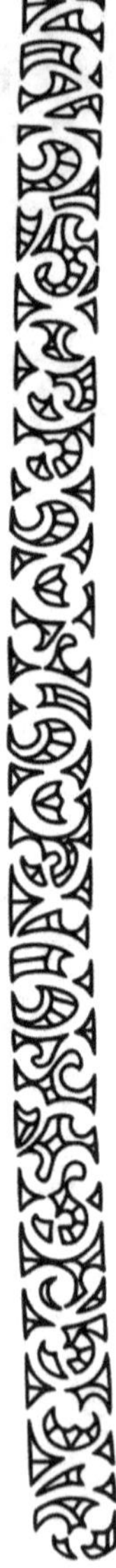

[4]   **Sun-moon**

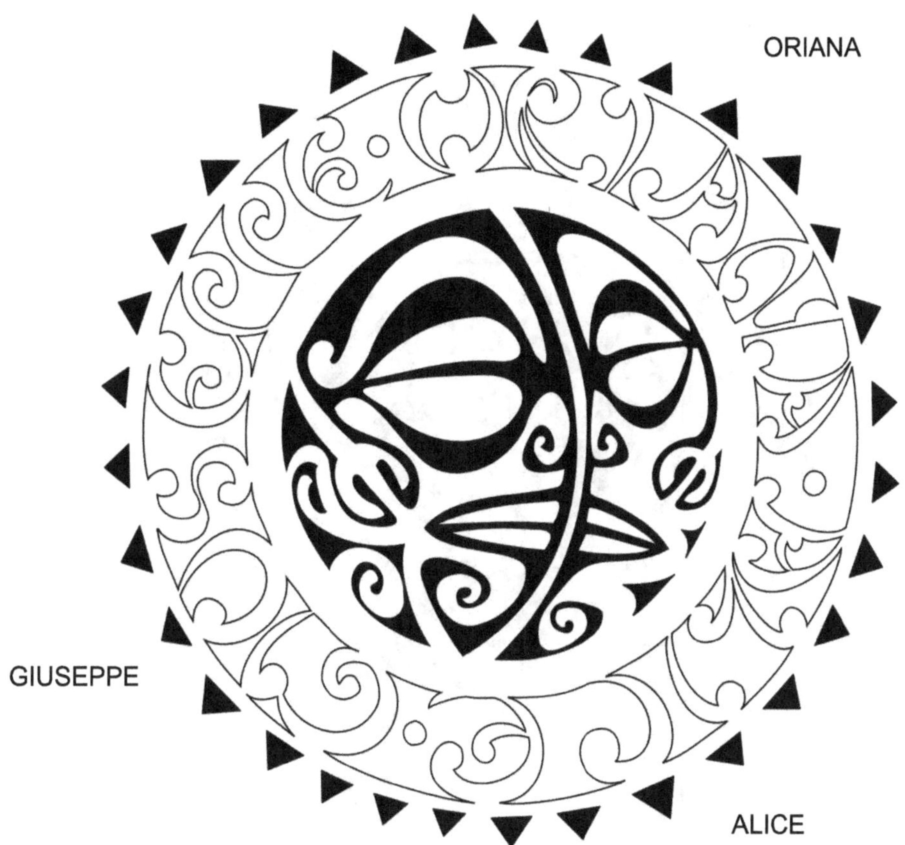

[5] **Balboa turtle**

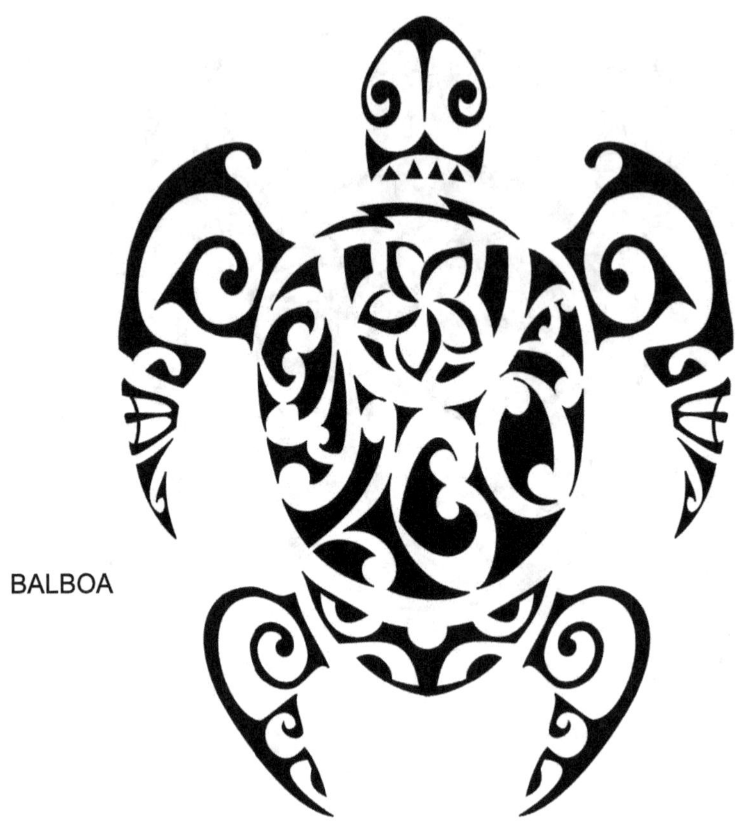

BALBOA

Tattoo traditions of Hawaii - *T. Allen: Mutual, 2006*

The journals of Captain Cook on his voyages of discovery - *J.C Beaglehole: The Hakluyt Society, 1967*

Polynesians: Prehistory of an Island People (Ancient Peoples and Places) - *P. Bellwood: Thames & Hudson, 1987*

Tattoos from Paradise: traditional Polynesian patterns - *M. Blackburn: Schiffer Publishing Ltd, 1999*

Oceanic Mythology - *Roland B. Dixon: Forgotten Books, 2010 reprint of 1916 edition*

An account of the Polynesian race: Its origin and migrations, and the ancient history of the Hawaiian people to the times of Kamehameha I - *A.Fornander; General Books reprint, 2010*

Wrapping in images: tattooing in Polynesia - *A. Gell: Clarendon Press, 1993*

Tattooing in the Marquesas - *W.C. Handy: B.P.Bishop Museum Bulletin no.1, 1922*

The Pacific Arts of Polynesia and Micronesia - *A.L. Kaeppler: Oxford University Press, 2008*

Adorning the World: Art of the Marquesas Islands - *E. Kjellgren and C.S. Ivory: Metropolitan Museum of Art, 2005*

The Hawaiian tattoo - *P.F. Kwiatkowski: Halona Inc., 1996*

Moko or Maori Tattooing - *H.G. Robley: Chapman and Hall Ltd, 1896*

L' art du tatouage aux îles Marquises - *K. Von den Steinen trad. par Denise et Robert Koenig: Haere Po, 2007*

TattooTribes.com
2011